CHERYL SUMMERS

The Curse

A True Story

Pacific Press®
Publishing Association

Nampa, Idaho | Oshawa, Ontario, Canada
www.pacificpress.com

Cover design by Steve Lanto
Cover design resources from istockphoto.com/Rastan, istockphoto.com/cassinga
Inside design by Aaron Troia

The author assumes full responsibility for the accuracy of all facts and quotations as cited in this book.

Most of the names used in this book are pseudonyms. Real names were used with permission.

Additional copies of this book are available by calling toll-free 1-800-765-6955 or by visiting http://www.AdventistBookCenter.com.

Library of Congress Cataloging-in-Publication Data
Names: Summers, Cheryl, author.
Title: The curse : a true story / Cheryl Summers.
Description: Nampa : Pacific Press Publishing Association, 2018.
Identifiers: LCCN 2017044127 | ISBN 9780816363131 (pbk. : alk. paper)
Subjects: LCSH: Summers, Cheryl. | Seventh-day Adventist converts—United
   States—Biography. | Occultism—Religious aspects—Christianity. |
   Spiritualism.
Classification: LCC BX6189.S86 A3 2018 | DDC 286.7092 [B]—dc23 LC record available at https://lccn.loc.gov/2017044127

November 2017

CONTENTS

DEDICATION

I dedicate this book with gratitude to author and speaker Chuck Wall, founder of Kindness Inc., who was the first to say this book needed to be written; to my daughter and son, who graciously said yes to the writing of this book; to Moms, Pops, Yolan, Reiner, and the ladies in my Bible study groups who have steadfastly carried me through this project with prayer and encouragement; to my stellar proofreaders, Ruth and Marie; and to Sally, who spent hours at my side going through the entire manuscript line by line. Love and thanks to you all.

PROLOGUE

ooking down at Rachel, with her soft, raven-colored hair gently curling at the ends; cherubic face still; and eyes closed in sleep, it was hard to believe she was almost one and a half years old. She was just an infant when I married Carl and moved from California to Idaho and into the little house he had rented for our family of three. Now almost a year later, we owned a brand-new split-level, two-bedroom home, bought with help from our folks and a low-interest government loan.

Rachel's room was large enough for a dresser, a wooden doll high chair from my childhood, a child's rocker, and a comfy full-sized mattress with sloping sides. There was no box spring or bed frame. The mattress sat flat on the plush blue carpeting. That way if Rachel—a very inquisitive child—crawled out from under the covers and over the side, she wouldn't fall as she had nearly done more than once from her crib. If she got adventurous, she would safely roll a few gentle inches down a padded incline to the carpet.

Gently brushing a stray hair from her face, I marveled that sleep was the only time she was truly quiet. Satisfied she would now stay asleep, I tiptoed out, leaving the door ajar, and turned out the light before padding quietly down the hall to the living room.

It was after 8:00 p.m. Carl was working late at Sears in the hardware department as a salesclerk. The house was still. Floor heaters kept the house warm; but when I pressed my nose to the big picture window, the glass felt icy. The dim glow from the stove's light in the nearby kitchen and the single living-room lamp cast dark shadows. Peering outside, I could barely make out the snowflakes drifting to the frozen ground below. The new snow muffled the sounds from our hilly suburban street.

I picked up a needlepoint project, sat in the rocker, and switched on the radio. We didn't own a TV. We had given Carl's old one away. While I had grown up watching TV, shows now seemed too worldly for my baby Christian eyes. Eliminating TV seemed like a grand and noble idea at the time, especially when the long summer evenings were filled with sunshine, gardening, and long walks. But dark winter nights made the house feel barren and empty. To fill the void and ward off fear, I often listened to campy old-time radio dramas whenever Carl worked late. They were entertaining and eased my loneliness. Of course, with all the fights we had been having lately, being alone was sometimes a welcome reprieve.

When we had married, it was with trepidation on my part. I was an unwed mother, raising an infant alone. Carl, who was not the father, had been my close friend long before Rachel arrived. Though I had always loved Carl, I was never *in love* with him. I had hoped that his intense love for me would someday spark a mutual romantic attraction. It had not. His heart and pride daily paid the price while mine grew harder in reaction to his angry outbursts. We were a broken mess of sharp pieces. I doubted we would ever be a happy, harmonious whole. Only Rachel's need for a cohesive family life and my own determination to not disappoint God kept me from walking away.

Shaking off my mental cobwebs, I realized a mystery was just starting. It sounded like a good one. Ending my reverie, I focused on the story while making stitches of gold-colored yarn to fill in the prestamped-canvas design of an old-fashioned girl reading by firelight. The single lamp wasn't enough, so I brought the canvas closer to see where the needle went next. While the mystery unfolded, my young, nimble fingers made each stitch perfect, just as my mother had instilled upon me when I first learned to do needlepoint: *always strive to be perfect.* The spell of concentration didn't break until an ominous cliff-hanger segued into a commercial for an age-spot cream—just what I needed at the age of twenty-one.

Momentarily distracted, I set the canvas down. My eyes swept the sparse room that contained used furniture and knickknacks from our youth. Assuming we would stay together, I wondered how long it would be before we could decorate the place like a real home. I yearned for comfy seating, good lighting, and artwork to liven up the walls. For now, the room's only real feature was a black cast-iron woodstove Carl had gotten from work. It didn't even burn wood; we couldn't afford to install a chimney.

I told myself it was OK to be young and poor, as long as we weren't poor forever. Carl's mother, an entertainment lawyer, came from a wealthy family in Los Angeles. His dad was a successful doctor in our small Idaho town. My debt-free parents lived just miles from Malibu, California, on

Dad's salary as a nuclear physicist and Mom's job as a college dean. We both came from disciplined, hardworking professional stock; yet neither of us had, at least so far, finished college or chosen a career.

Before coming to Idaho and going into retail sales, Carl had spurned his grandfather's offer to set him up in the family asphalt business. I helped out by providing day care but couldn't charge much in our blue-collar town. We lived paycheck to paycheck, as victims of our own poor choices and stubborn scrappiness. By forgoing a degree and a helping hand, we had trapped ourselves in financial hardship.

The commercial ended and the dramatic music swelled. The characters started talking again, accentuated by the creaking of door hinges and the *clomp, clomp* of heavy footsteps.

I glanced back down at my handiwork but immediately noticed the design was harder to see than before. The gloomy room had grown darker, as if someone had dimmed the lights. Unnerved, I set the needlework aside and turned off the radio, straining my ears for any odd sounds. I looked around for anything out of place that might explain the situation.

From the chair, I could hear the refrigerator humming and the clock above the dining table ticking. Somewhere outside, our dogs barked. The back kitchen door, partly visible, was closed and locked. The front door at the bottom of the unlit entry stairs was beyond my line of sight but still close enough to hear if anyone opened it. No one had. Downstairs the basement had two windows big enough for someone to crawl through, but no errant sounds came from that direction either. The house seemed secure. Yet something was very wrong. A feeling of evil filled the air, replacing the relative peace of the moments before. This was a feeling I had experienced before—years ago.

A minute ticked by as I held my body taut like a piano string. Gradually, the house grew darker still, despite the lights remaining on. Then it started. One after another, out-of-place sounds echoed down the hall, emanating from one of the bedrooms. The danger was imminent, palpable, and obvious. Fear filled my gut with a sickening wave as my thoughts flew back in time to when I was a teenager and had just left the occult for Jesus. My friend Hal, who led me to Christ, had warned me back then that Satan might someday go after my children. Was Hal's warning now coming true? Standing up, I forced my steps forward and headed back down the hall toward Evil.

CHAPTER

1

By the time I graduated high school in 1976, I was convinced I was living with a ghost. It had taken over my bedroom, which was actually a separate, oval-shaped guesthouse perched on a cliff about fifty yards in front of my parents' lakeside 1930s home near Malibu. The lakefront was a small, artsy community made up of actors, musicians, and other quirky professionals who spurned conformity. It was a Tinsel Town, hippie haven where the residents agreed to live and let live. Having a resident ghost was not all that unusual there, and it fit right in with my lifelong fascination with the occult. In the Girl Scouts, we frequently indulged in séances during sleepovers, told ghost stories, and levitated each other. I loved watching spooky TV shows late at night and reading books about ghost towns, haunted houses, and witchcraft, so I was excited to have a ghost of my own—at least in the beginning.

Most times the appearance of the ghost was like the wind. No one could see the actual ghost, but we all saw the effects it had on everything in the room. Lights or the radio would turn on and off at will. A hanging plant would sway in circles without a breeze. Objects, from keys in my purse to entire baskets of clothes, would disappear from the guesthouse and later reappear somewhere else. Unseen fingers rapped on the TV's metal housing one night in an angry tempo to chase away my best friend Sara. The inside curtain of the front door would sometimes pull back when I slipped the key in the lock, as if someone inside wanted to know who was there. The dog sometimes trembled as she looked around the room, though nothing seemed amiss. More than once, I was suddenly accosted by loud pounding on the walls that made the room shake. Worst of all, I suffered nightly attacks when the ghost would startle me awake with paralyzing, vicious strength.

Despite all that, I only saw the ghost twice. The first time was early in the morning. I should have been up, getting ready for summer school.

Instead, I had slept in. I awoke to the sensation that someone was watching me. I opened my eyes, and a handsome young man with longish brown hair and arresting blue eyes was beside the bed, smiling, with his arm outstretched in invitation. I gazed back, amazed, wondering who he could be. I stretched out a hand, and he took it, gently pulling me up and out of bed. I stood for a second, staring into his captivating eyes. He was enchanting; I couldn't wait to talk with him and get to know him. Then like a cruel mirage, he was instantly gone. I was standing there, staring into the empty space where he had stood just seconds before.

The second time was in the middle of the night. Sara had stayed for a sleepover, and she slept beside me in bed. I woke up suddenly, horrified because this time the ghost was sitting on top of me, holding me down. His blue eyes were dark with rage and stared down into mine, not smiling. I couldn't move or speak. I struggled to wrestle him off, wondering why Sara didn't wake up and help me. Then, in an instant, he was gone. I could move again. Next to me Sara still slept. Terrified, it took me several hours to go back to sleep.

Whether seen or unseen, ghosts rarely come uninvited. My friends and I had greatly encouraged this ghost's presence by playing with an Ouija board; holding séances; experimenting with drugs, such as marijuana and various pills; and drinking alcohol. I often listened to heavy-metal rock music with dark, mystical lyrics. The most tantalizing of all was discovering that Sara lived next door to the actress who played the witch Samantha on *Bewitched*, spurring Sara and I on to explore the mysteries of the spirit realm even more.

At first, it was fun having a ghost around. It didn't take long, though, for things to get crazy, with increasingly terrifying occurrences happening in my room and beyond. I just wanted the ghost to leave, but it wouldn't. Unable to cope, I left home on my eighteenth birthday, returning to the San Fernando Valley where my parents, Chuck and Dorothy, had raised me until we bought the lake house.

In order to afford moving out, I got financial aid, registered for classes at the community college where Mom was the dean of college development, and worked in the campus library. I rented a room from a single mom and her son in a comfortable, newer home that should have been ghost free. Within weeks, the ghost crossed many miles to inhabit that space as well.

At first, only I knew it was there. Then one weekend when I slept at a friend's house, the ghost retaliated by scaring my landlord all night with banging noises outside her bedroom and destroying my room, knocking things over and tearing keepsakes from the wall.

That first night back, after I cleaned up the mess and went to bed, the room suddenly reverberated with the ghost's hideous laughter, which lasted several minutes and was loud enough to be heard throughout the house. The next day I was told to move.

By Christmas, I was sharing a converted garage with my friend Crystal. The ghost went there, too, and soon chased poor Crystal out.

I couldn't afford to stay there alone, so in the spring of 1977, I moved back to the lake. For fifty dollars a month, I lived with my friend Julie; her mother, Ellie; her younger brother Tim; and her older brother, Kurt, whom I'd dated in high school, in their rambling two-story house. It was a great house, built by film star Clark Gable for his weekend hunting excursions. It sat high on the mountainside above the lake and had a TV studio's back lot on the other side, where *M*A*S*H* was still being filmed.

Like other homes in the area, the Gable house boasted its own ghost, which was famous for scaring people and animals alike. I was curious about this "new" ghost, so the first time I went there as a young teenager, I demanded out loud that it show itself. It took months, but it finally showed up late one night.

Kurt and I were sharing an easy chair in the living room after a party. As he talked, I absently gazed out of one of the room's many windows that looked out on the second-story veranda. Suddenly, a young woman appeared to walk up the outside steps, stopping in front of a window. Her face was clearly visible in the soft glow of the table lamp near the window. She was beautiful, wore an antiquated Spanish dress, and had her long, dark hair swept up in ringlet curls. She slowly turned her head and looked inside; her eyes locked on mine and a slow, intent smile emerged. I stared back, wondering if I knew her. I turned to tell Kurt, who laughed. When I looked back a second later, she was gone. We immediately went outside to investigate. Kurt was quick to point out that the window was so high above the flagstone steps that she would have had to be twelve feet tall in order to look in. Impossible.

Now, almost two years after that strange encounter, I was living in that house. And so, we soon realized, was my ghost. The combination of the two ghosts in one household was too much. When my classes ended for the summer, I moved back home to the guesthouse and back to square one. Nothing had changed. In fact, it only got worse and was about to come to a head.

After a day at the beach, I was driving Julie and myself home in Ellie's red Pontiac Firebird. It was nearly nightfall. When we drove past an empty park between the lake and the mountain, we both suddenly saw what appeared to be a severed female head in the middle of the road, with the face turned upward, mouth and eyes wide open, and hair tangled in all directions. It looked as if the person had been killed midscream. Startled, I almost hit a tree when I tried to avoid running over the specter.

By the time I regained control of the car and was past the head, Julie spun around to look out the back. "It's gone!" she yelped, gripping the seat with both hands.

I circled the park to look for traces of the head, including blood on the road or signs of mischievous kids playing a prank. We found nothing. The park and roads were empty, so we gave up and drove on to Julie's house.

Racing up the steps to the veranda, we burst through the front door and told Ellie what we had seen, unaware that we were interrupting her date with Hal. Ellie, dressed casually in jeans, sat on the worn-out sofa looking stunned. Hal sat quietly in a nearby chair but, unlike Ellie, didn't look shocked at all. Instead, he merely brushed back his strawberry-blond hair and listened. When we finally stopped talking, Hal questioned us about using the Ouija board and other occult practices. Julie stayed quiet, letting me answer.

"I can help you, girls, if you want," he said.

Julie's eyes locked on a small Bible in Hal's shirt pocket and vigorously shook her head. "Not me. I'm going to bed. Good night." She walked away, then slammed her bedroom door.

I was suspicious of Hal's Bible, too, but I was desperate. "How?" I asked. "We've tried everything, even a parapsychologist."

Hal remained unfazed. "Ellie, would you mind if Cheryl and I talked privately in the kitchen?"

"Sure," she said, running a hand through her short, red hair. "I'll just do some reading." She reached for a paperback on the coffee table.

I nervously followed Hal to the kitchen and sat across from him at the table. He pulled out the Bible and slid it to me. I had been raised without church or religion by parents who were staunch atheistic evolutionists. My mother, an anthropologist, thought the world was millions of years old. My father saw the world in tangible terms of math and physics, leaving no room for Creation or God. I had never read a Bible. I was an unchurched heathen. Naturally, I eyed the black book skeptically, not knowing anything about God, Evil, the Christmas story, or anything else contained in its sacred text.

Undaunted, Hal pointed to a page near the beginning. "Read it out loud."

I read from Genesis about Creation and the fall of man. It was in English, but the words were perplexing. They also stirred up an unexpected, unexplainable rage. I felt agitated and uncomfortable, as if plunged into deep waters with no idea of how to swim. There seemed to be no obvious connection between the story I was reading and the severed head in the road.

"What does this have to do with *anything* that happened tonight?" I exploded, slamming the book shut. "This is just a stupid story about a snake. You promised to help me! Julie was right."

"I *am* helping you," he said patiently. He explained that the snake was Satan, a supreme angel who was kicked out of heaven with many other angels, resulting in demons that roamed the earth in search of prey. He said demons commonly paraded as the ghosts of dead strangers or loved ones. "So you see, you don't have a ghost at all! They don't exist. You have a demon. And if you'll pray with me and follow some simple instructions, God will make the demon leave."

Hal's explanation was shockingly different from others I had heard: I was nuts; the ghost was a murder victim from the turn of the century; or, as the parapsychologist theorized, it was the negative energy of unseen beings. Making matters worse, the irrational anger I had felt while reading had only intensified with Hal's explanation. And prayer? I didn't know what that was!

Despite all this, I grudgingly repeated after him, uttering my first prayer, asking Jesus into my heart. Afterward, Hal told me to destroy any occult paraphernalia or drugs in the guesthouse.

"Get sober; drugs are an open invitation to demons," he said. "Get to know Jesus by reading the Bible and praying. And find a church as soon as possible."

It was a tall order that sounded bizarre. But because nothing else had worked, I had to try. I left with Hal's Bible, some instructions, and lots of doubts. I had seen demons with my own eyes, so I figured God had to be real too. I would fake it till I could make it.

* * * * *

The next day I threw away my marijuana, books on haunted houses, and music by rock groups such as Black Sabbath. Days later, I destroyed the main culprit—the Ouija board—which took hours to burn. I started and ended each day by reading aloud the prayer Hal had helped me write out. I even slept with the Bible.

Ellie, already a sober member of Alcoholics Anonymous (AA), took me to several meetings and tagged along as I tried out various churches. This was a spiritual battle for my life, and I knew it.

In time, the demon's ghostlike antics trickled to a stop. Inanimate objects stayed put, and radios didn't turn on by themselves. But nearly every night I was still attacked while sleeping. Thankfully, I knew how to stop the demonic attacks when they hit; Hal told me to speak the name of Jesus out loud. (Luke 10:17 says demons are subject to His name.) The problem was getting the attacks to stop. The guesthouse was clean. There was nothing left to throw away or burn.

Out of frustration, I asked Carl for advice. We had met at a young people's AA meeting and became good friends. He was tall and thin, with pale skin and dark hair and eyes, and was cute in a boy-next-door kind of way. He was adventurous, fun, and generous to a fault, but I wasn't attracted to him.

"Give me time," he said. "I'll ask around."

Days later he had a plan. "Someone told me about a group in Pasadena. They help people that have evil spirits. They're holding a meeting tonight if you want to go. I'll pay."

"Carl, I don't have *spirits*. It's a demon."

"Whatever. At least give it a shot."

I was reluctant but agreed. I needed my nights back. That evening in the waning August light, we drove through heavy traffic on the Ventura Freeway in his worn-out Pinto, arriving late. We quickly checked in and paid, then a man took us to seats along the back wall of the meeting room.

I sat beside a middle-aged woman who looked at me knowingly.

"Hi," she said, patting my hand. "I'm Madge. I understand you're having ghost troubles."

Surprised, I blinked in confusion. "Sort of," I admitted. "How did you know?"

"Don't worry," Madge said, flashing an encouraging smile. "I'll explain later. We just want to help! You'll see. *Shh*, the speaker is getting ready to start. We'll talk afterward." Madge folded her hands submissively and focused her attention on the speaker at the mic.

I aimed a quizzical look at Carl. He just shrugged and faced the front.

"Hello, ladies and gentlemen. My name is Clarisse. Tonight I'll share with you the secrets to getting everything your heart desires!" Clarisse's bright eyes scanned the room, then landed on me. She gave me a slow, intimate smile, which conveyed secret delight. She looked over at Madge, who nodded, then gazed at me one more time before turning to the crowd at large and holding up a large white Bible.

"This is the secret. Yes, the Bible! I know you're thinking this is a meeting, not a revival, right? Let me assure you; this is *not* church! I'm here to introduce you to the ancient art of white magic. What is that, you ask? White magic combines incantations that tap into the enormous, limitless power of nature, the universe, and the spirit realm with Holy Scripture from the Bible. When you put these two powerful things together, watch out! There's nothing you can't do or have. Let me explain . . ."

This time I turned to Carl accusingly. The mere mention of magic was raising huge red flags, but he kept his eyes aimed at the speaker and ignored me.

For thirty minutes, Clarisse wrote incantations and Bible verses on a blackboard, explaining which ones worked together best for getting a new car, finding love, being healed from disease, or creating wealth. The crowd seemed excited by this revolutionary information, asking questions and scribbling notes. Meanwhile, I silently wondered if this was a huge mistake. I didn't understand white magic any more than I did the Bible, but it didn't sound right. But we had paid, so we stayed.

Clarisse wrapped up the meeting by reminding everyone there would be another one next week with even more powerful information. Stepping back from the podium, she shook several hands, then walked with purpose to the back of the room, straight to us.

"Hi there," she said, proffering her hand. "I'm Clarisse. What's your name?"

"Cheryl," I mumbled, shaking her hand before finding my own jeans pocket.

Clarisse shook Carl's hand and then turned back to me. "Did you enjoy the meeting? Wouldn't *you* like to have everything you want, when you want it?"

I shrugged, not knowing what to say.

"Well, never mind. We can talk more about that later. Tonight I think we'd better see about getting rid of those evil spirits that keep bothering you!"

Again I was stunned. Carl hadn't said anything to the man at the registration table. How did these women know about the demon? More important, could they really get rid of it completely?

As if reading my mind, Madge leaned forward and spoke in quiet, conspiratorial tones. "Don't be alarmed that we know. When a person has evil spirits, it shows in her aura."

"My *what?*"

"Your *aura*. The energy your inner being gives off." Madge nodded knowingly at Clarisse. "Those gifted with supernatural powers, as Clarisse and I are, can easily read your aura to see what's going on."

"Yes," Clarisse agreed. "But for now, just tell us if you want our help. We can rid you of those spirits tonight. It won't take long. We have a private room in the back. What do you say? Shall we go?"

I signaled Carl with my eyes to make some excuse to leave immediately. He just offered a weak smile. "I can wait here while you go with them."

Traitor, I thought. I was trapped. Something told me this was risky business, but I couldn't think of a single reason to say No. They were being so kind. Ever the people pleaser, I didn't want to hurt their feelings.

"OK," I agreed, letting them lead me to a small back room. It had a tall, narrow table with a cushion on top. Next to that a short, square table held a fat candle and a meager lamp, which was the room's only light. Clarisse lit the candle with a match and switched off the lamp.

Madge shut and locked the door. "We don't want anyone interrupting!" she said, smiling as she pushed her short, mousy-brown hair out of her eyes. Then she was at my side. "Stretch out on the table, and make yourself comfy," she instructed, lowering her voice to a whisper. "That's it. Just lie back and relax."

When I was settled, Clarisse positioned herself on the other side of the table; her long gray curls swaying as she moved. Both women started mumbling unintelligible words and phrases, and their voices grew in intensity. Clarisse took the candle and, with alternating hands, swept it back and forth mere inches above the length of my body from head to toe, over and over.

Reaching over, Madge gently stroked my forehead. "Close your eyes, dear," she said with a hushed, intense voice. "That's right. *Shh.*"

Clarisse continued moving the candle up and down my body; her hands hovered close to my skin but never touched it. Despite the lack of physical contact, I keenly felt each sweep of the candle as my skin and muscles grew warm, then uncomfortably hot. I could feel and hear Madge swaying nearby and moaning. Clarisse's voice grew louder, but her words remained foreign to me. At the same time, my mind grew fuzzy and I experienced a floating sensation. I felt drugged. Whatever they were doing was powerful, and I'd had enough.

"Are we almost done?" I asked, opening my eyes and searching their candlelit faces. Their eyes looked wild in the midst of this strange, frightening ritual.

With noticeable effort, Madge refocused her eyes on mine and offered a strange smile. "Of course," she said, "*Shh.* We're almost finished." She reached over and smoothed my arms and legs with soft, intimate touches, even as she ever-so-slightly pushed me downward to keep me on the table. Then she placed both hands gently yet firmly on my right arm and closed her eyes, resuming her swaying and mumbling in a quieter voice.

I looked at Clarisse. Her eyes met mine briefly, then she carefully set down the candle. Closing her eyes halfway, she, too, began rubbing my limbs one by one and smoothing my hair. I had never been comfortable being touched by strangers, and this was no exception. I was ready to bolt.

Clarisse must have felt my body tensing. "Ah," she breathed out a moment later. "Yes, that's it, yes." She opened her eyes all the way and stared down at me intently, almost lovingly, then gently took my hands in hers. "You are cleansed," she said softly. "We have taken all the evil energy out of you. Here, let me help you sit up. That's it; slowly, not too fast or you may faint."

With help, I carefully got down from the table. My skin was starting to cool, but my entire being felt woozy and out of balance, like waking from a deep sleep.

"I feel strange," I admitted.

"It will pass," Madge said.

"Of course, it will," Clarisse cooed, while handing me a packet of white powder. "You'll be fine. Now take this home, and pour it into a cast-iron skillet. Light it and wave it in the air as you walk through your house. Let the smoke fill the space as you repeat these incantations. Here, they're all written out."

"What for?" I asked, taking the paper.

"We cleansed *you.* Now you must cleanse your *house.* And don't wait, do it tonight."

We left the room, and I found Carl waiting in the same chair by the wall. Back in the car, I told him everything that had happened.

"You're going to do it, right?" he asked.

"Only if you do it with me."

"Sure. We've come this far. Might as well finish the job."

An hour later I lit the powder in my mother's skillet and held it out in front of us as we chanted the strange words on the paper Clarisse had given me. They made no sense, so after two trips around the room, including the closet and bathroom, we stopped.

"That's enough," I said. "Let's open the windows to let out the smoke."

"Do you know what those words mean?" he asked.

"No. They just said this would cleanse the house of evil spirits." I looked at him warily. "Where did you hear about this group?"

"A guy at a meeting. Are you sorry we went?"

"I just think it was weird. But hey, if it works, I won't complain! It's late; you'd better go."

After he left, I got ready for bed and read Hal's prayer aloud. Turning out the light, I breathed in the warm, pine-laced air and listened to the familiar nocturnal sounds of ducks, frogs, owls, and coyotes as I gradually drifted off to sleep.

CHAPTER

2

In the darkness, I slipped easily into a pleasant dream.

Suddenly, all peace shattered as something jerked me awake. I immediately felt the familiar, viselike paralysis of a demonic attack. Similar to previous episodes, the room took on an eerie glow. Everything was slightly out of focus, including the bank of multipaned windows across from the bed, which faced the lake and the surrounding mountains. Framed by filmy, purple curtains, the windows moved as one animal-like unit, lunging at me in menacing unison before retreating to where they belonged, only to lunge again. The entire room was charged with an electric energy as an unseen being held me down in the bed with a steel grip. I struggled to move, to break free, but the force pressing me down was too powerful to resist.

The intensity of this attack was different. It was explosively worse than any that had come before, like a thunderstorm ramped up to a hurricane. It felt like a runaway train was upon me, allowing no escape, making it hard to breathe and nearly impossible to move or speak. As a vicious, elusive enemy aimed a ton of wicked power directly at my frail humanity, death didn't just feel possible, it felt inevitable and unstoppable.

Shocked and exhausted, I stopped fighting for a brief second to gather strength and get my bearings. That was a mistake! In that swift sliver of time, the demon unleashed an even higher level of fury. I felt as though this fight was over. The enemy was too strong. Inwardly, I conceded that I would die in that bed—and would be killed by something I couldn't see. Yet even as I despaired, in the chaos I remembered that all I had to do was gather enough strength to say the name of Jesus aloud. This battle was not mine to win. It was His! With a deep breath, I stopped fighting and focused all my energy on speaking His name. At first, no sound came out; I wasn't even sure my mouth was moving. Then, like a woman in the final throes of labor, I pushed one more time with all that I had, straining to open my mouth and force air from my lungs, past the vocal cords to the room beyond.

"Jes . . . ," the broken sound escaped my lips, then "Jesus!"

Instantly, the spell broke. Like a taut rubber band, the room snapped back to normal in every way. The windows were placidly still, lit only by soft moonlight. The room's ominous energy neutralized. The pressure on my chest vanished. I could move freely. Even the sheets appeared undisturbed. The room bore no trace of what had just occurred. I, on the other hand, was drenched in sweat, breathing hard like a runner after a race. I had survived the battle. Could I endure more? I didn't think so.

I turned on the light, grabbed my pink princess phone, and called a very sleepy Hal.

"Cheryl, it's three in the morning. What's going on?"

I quickly poured out the details of the strange evening and the severity of this latest attack.

"You did *what?*" he yelled. "Are you *kidding* me? That's insane! You know the definition of insanity, right? Doing the same thing and expecting different results. Why in God's name would you go to a meeting of witches? I told you to stay *away* from anything demonic!"

Stricken by his words, I started to cry.

"Did you *really* not understand what you were doing?" he asked more gently.

"No. They had Bibles! They wrote verses on the board."

He snorted. "Big deal, they had Bibles. Here's a verse for you: 'Even the demons believe—and tremble!' [James 2:19, NKJV]. Just because someone waves a Bible around doesn't mean she serves God. A witch is a witch, no matter how many scriptures she quotes. And witches serve Satan. They *deceived* you."

"I know," I whispered. "But I did everything you told me to do, and the demon kept attacking me, night after night. I had to do something; I needed help!"

"Well, you went to the wrong place."

"Obviously. But this attack was *so* bad! What should I do?"

There was silence, then he cleared his throat. "I guess I'm going to have to come over and fix this. But not tonight. I'll come tomorrow after the five o'clock meeting."

"What am I supposed to do tonight?"

"You have the Bible. Read it. Keep a light on if it helps. You'll be OK; morning will come."

I pulled the Bible from beneath the sheets. For hours, I doggedly read until dawn turned the windows pink. Feeling safe at last, I fell into a deep, undisturbed sleep.

* * * * *

The next evening my parents and I sat like disconnected islands, eating dinner on trays, with the TV blaring. Dad was in his recliner and had a glass of wine on the end table. I sat in a matching recliner, also facing the TV. Mom was at the dining table in front of the windows overlooking the sundeck and pine trees.

Hal was coming soon. I knew my parents would wonder why an older man was coming to visit me. As I pushed ham and rice around my plate, I decided to tell them what was going on. I also had something to confess.

In high school, I had tried to tell them about the ghost. It was the only way to explain why I had lost house keys or didn't hear the buzzer ring when they needed me in the main house. Instead of believing me, they punished me. When that didn't work, they took me to a psychiatrist. He declared me sane and then explained that I was acting out from Dad's drinking, Mom's long work hours, and my fears of sleeping alone, triggering an overactive imagination that manifested in perceived ghosts. I knew he was wrong, but I played along in order to get out of trouble. After that, I said nothing more to them about the ghost. That had been the year before.

Now that I was back in the guesthouse, understood the ghost was a demon, and had gotten it to leave me alone during waking hours, I thought I should tell my parents the truth, even though they might think I was crazy.

"Dad," I said, nervous about interrupting his show.

"*Hmm?*" he said, giving me an annoyed look as he chewed, then turning back to the show.

I looked at Mom for support. Her benign gaze was fixed on a library book. I tried again. "Dad, you know that painting I gave you for Father's Day?"

He pulled his attention from the TV with noticeable irritation. "Yeah. What about it?"

"Well, when you were away on your trip last week, I . . . burned it. It's gone."

His expression turned surprised and then stony. I expected him to yell or slam his fist on the table as he had done in the past—always the accuser, never the gentle listener. I waited. He sipped his wine and turned toward the office where the painting had hung and then back to me.

"I hadn't noticed. Why did you burn it?"

I had painted it for a college art class that spring. It was good but exuded a dark presence from its inception. I had painted it in the converted garage I shared with Crystal, working for days perched on a stool before an easel, trying to finish in time for the class to critique. While I was painting, loud banging noises emanated from around the room, and unseen hands kept knocking me off the stool and upsetting the canvas. Angry at the ornery "ghost," I yelled at it to stop and kept painting.

The finished work was black, white, and gray oils on canvas. It depicted two men sleeping beneath a large, wrinkly parachute, their heads beside each other's feet like a diagonal 69, creating a ying-and-yang effect. The man in the lighter half of the image had light hair and a peaceful expression; his half of the parachute was brightly lit. His counterpart had dark hair, a menacing expression, and lay in shadow.

At the critique, the students and teacher said it made them uncomfortable. One girl jumped and then claimed she had seen the expression of one of the sleeping men move, as if the ghost had added supernatural animation to the finished piece. The disturbed looks of the class carried judgment and suspicion.

"I think it's evil," one girl proclaimed. The teacher did not correct her.

I didn't understand then what evil was. I just knew I didn't want to paint anymore. I was afraid of what my hands might create next.

Not knowing what else to do with it, I gave it to Dad, hoping it would fit in with his odd mix of nudes, jungle scenes, and abstract images. He acted happy with it and hung it in the office right away. But I soon noticed that whenever I went in there, the image stared back menacingly, like a living portrait of two spirits. So when Hal told me to burn the Ouija board, I knew that painting had to go too.

I was relieved it was gone. It had been the right thing to do. Now I just had to convince Dad.

"Dad, the painting bothered me every time I looked at it. It bothered other people too. A lot."

He sat quietly, not smiling. Meanwhile, Mom stopped reading to watch us both. To my surprise, he nodded benignly. "I know," he agreed. "I didn't say anything at the time, but it bothered me too. That's why I hung it in there, instead of out here with your other paintings."

"So you're not mad?"

"No. But you should have asked before you did it. It was mine, after all."

"Of course! I'm sorry I didn't." Gaining courage, I plunged on. "Dad, the reason I've been going to church and meetings and stuff is because the ghost I told you about last summer was getting really scary. You see, Hal explained it wasn't a ghost at all; it was a demon. I know you don't believe in God, so you probably don't believe in demons either. But I think that's what was wrong with the painting. A demon harassed me the whole time I worked on it. I think it even became part of the painting!"

He stared back, with his mouth a straight line. Then he got up, turned off the TV, and sat back down. "Ghosts?" he spat out, astounded. "I thought we were through with all that nonsense!"

"No," I said. "It *never* stopped, not even when I moved out last fall."

When he didn't argue, I shared what had gone on in the rented room, the converted garage, and the frightening experiences that had led up to the head in the road.

"The demon isn't gone completely," I admitted. "So Hal is coming over in a little while to help."

My parents eyed each other and then me. "Is that why you're suddenly so religious?" he asked. "And this Hal guy, he's religious too?"

I nodded, pretending not to notice the slight roll of his eyes.

"It sounds crazy to me," he said, taking another sip. Then his gaze grew distant, as his thoughts drifted back in time. "You know to be fair, there was one time when I thought I heard angels outside my bedroom window. Who knows? If angels can visit an ornery kid like me, maybe demons can exist too."

"Really?" I asked, amazed. "What happened?"

"I don't really know. I was just a kid, living in Michigan with my family. Back then, we all went to church. Anyway, I'd been in bed for days with a fever. One afternoon I heard voices singing right outside. It was beautiful. We lived by the woods. No neighbors nearby. My family was all in the next room talking. So I figured it had to be angels."

"Wow! That's cool, Dad."

He shrugged. "If you say so. Anyway, right after that, the fever broke and I got well."

"Then why don't you believe in God?"

"It's just not scientific! I need more proof than that. But hey, believe whatever you want. Just don't shove it down my throat."

I looked back at my mom. "What do you think?"

"I agree with him. I know you wouldn't lie about such things, but believing in God is another matter. I gave that up a long time ago. But do what makes *you* happy."

Just then a car drove up outside. "That's Hal. Thanks for dinner. I'll do dishes in the morning."

I met Hal coming up the stone pathway that led to the guesthouse. At the guesthouse door, I took in the glistening lake below, touched golden as the sun sank slowly behind the ring of mountains. Two boats sailed by, and children could be heard playing across the water. The sultry air was filled with the quacking of ducks and other sounds of summer. It was a deceptively peaceful evening.

"How did the rest of your night go?" Hal asked once we were inside.

"OK."

"No more problems?"

"No. I read the Bible till sunup and then I slept."

Hal flopped cross-legged on the carpeting, pointing to a spot three feet away. "Sit and face me."

I complied. "What are you going to do?"

"We aren't going to burn incense and chant incantations," he said sarcastically.

I blinked, chagrined afresh.

"Sorry; that was harsh," he admitted, softening his expression. "We're going to pray."

"Pray? That's all?"

" 'That's *all*?' What do you think prayer is? Look, there's a demon in this house, and prayer is the only way to get it out. There is *power* in prayer. You're going to have to trust me on that!"

"OK," I shrugged. "If you say so."

"I do. Now close your eyes and bow your head. I'll do the praying."

With that, Hal launched into a detailed prayer thanking God for His mercy and grace and sending Jesus to die on the cross to gain victory over death, Satan, and all his demons. Then Hal asked forgiveness for all that Carl and I had done the night before. As Hal spoke, I could feel the power of his words; but just as in Ellie's kitchen, I also felt unexplainable rage building up, threatening to spill out in a scream. I struggled to hold it in check by sheer will. Then his voice suddenly stopped. I kept my eyes shut, fists clenched, and mouth a tight line of fury.

"Open your eyes!"

When I did, my gaze met his with a defiant glare. He flinched but never looked away.

"Satan, in the name of Jesus, I command you to come out of her!" He looked straight at me. "Come out and go to dry places!"

Like a helpless puppet, I watched and listened as Hal's unexpected exorcism played out. I couldn't understand why my body wanted to lunge at him in hatred. I felt caught in the same evil force of energy that attacked me at night. Except now it was coming from *inside* of me, with the lights on and Hal as the target. I felt disconnected from my face, hands, and voice and torn apart by a battle raging, inside and outside my body, beyond my control.

"By the authority of Jesus, I order you to leave this house and never come back!" Hal demanded. Without warning, he suddenly looked terrified—which terrified me. Neither of us moved or looked away. "Go! In the name of Jesus, leave her!"

I shuddered as the rage left my body. My hands slowly unclenched, and my eyes and mouth relaxed.

"Thank You, Jesus," he said, watching me intently. "Thank You, Father, for her deliverance." Finally, he smiled. "Feel better?"

I nodded. "What happened?" I asked in bewilderment.

He let out a short, tense laugh. "Don't you know? A demon came out of you!"

My hand flew to my mouth. "What? There was a demon *inside me*? How do you know?"

"Because I saw him! Half your face was you, the other half the *demon*. And it was scary looking! But it's gone now."

Shaken, I tried to picture a demon face on my own. I couldn't. It was too awful.

"Thank you, Hal," I whispered sincerely. "I do feel better."

"We aren't done yet. Now it's *your* turn to pray. Repeat after me."

Gently, he led me through a prayer of confession, repentance, and thanksgiving for God's ability to rid me of the demon, restore my mind, and secure my salvation.

"Amen!" Hal proclaimed, giving me a quick hug and preparing to leave. "You know, that was my first exorcism. Can't say I want to do another one!"

"I'm so glad you came, Hal. Thanks again."

"You're welcome, kiddo," he said, back to his usual friendly self. "But there's one more thing."

"What?" I asked, afraid what he might do next.

"You know Satan's pretty angry about what happened here tonight. You've been under his control for a long time. Now you're free."

"So?"

"So he might want revenge."

"Revenge? Hasn't he tortured me enough?"

"I'm talking about your future children. He may go after *them* in order to get back at *you*."

I opened my mouth to object, but Hal raised a hand.

"I'm not saying he will, just that he might. Years from now, remember what I'm telling you. For now, no more messing with witchcraft! Find a church as fast as possible. That's your best protection."

* * * * *

For the rest of the summer, I visited more churches. Then I met a new friend at AA. Beth and I were the same age and height, and I loved her warm smile; long mane of curly, blond hair; and quirky view of life. We quickly became close friends. One afternoon she came up with an interesting plan.

"Want to do something different?" she asked.

"Depends. I never know with you," I teased.

"I just heard about a cool church. The Sunday evening service starts in a little bit. Want to go?"

I couldn't hide my surprise. Beth was the least religious person I knew. But I liked the idea of going together to visit a new church. That evening we heard a sermon on the power of prayer, then the pastor invited anyone who wanted to be baptized to come up to the platform.

Suddenly, Beth grabbed my hand and started pulling me up. "Come on, let's get baptized!"

I had no idea what that meant and felt sure I didn't want to do it. But Beth was so insistent and tugged so hard that I finally gave in, complaining all the way. A woman at the front told us to form a line and wait our turn. Panicking, I looked around and tried to understand what I had gotten myself into.

The next thing I knew, a man who was standing in the middle of a small pool was reaching for my hand. He put his arm around my shoulders and started praying, then gently pulled me down into the water until I was submerged, head and all. For a second, I felt scared at being unexpectedly underwater, but a second later, I was back up, standing beside him. He smiled and offered his congratulations, then led me to the other side of the pool where someone helped me climb out. I was all wet, with no idea why.

Beth went next. "Wasn't that great?" she asked, shaking water from her curls.

"Great? What *was* that?" I giggled. "Why are we all wet?"

"Because, silly, we were baptized! Now we'll get into heaven when we die."

The rest of the evening was a blur as others dried us off and then prayed over us again.

That night I relived it all in my head, trying to make sense of it. I still didn't understand it all but had to admit I felt a little different inside. According to one woman there, I now belonged to God. I hoped that was true, even if I didn't know what that meant. I was determined to find out someday.

Despite being baptized, I didn't go back to that church. It made me uncomfortable when people started weeping and praying in a strange language no one understood. In fact, I didn't like any of the churches I had visited so far.

When I ran into Hal at a meeting, I said something. "Hal, I've tried. Either the preacher wants everyone to say a bunch of weird stuff that sounds crazy, the sermon is boring and I don't understand it, or the people are old and dozing in the pews. Can't I just go to AA? I'm comfortable in meetings."

Hal sympathetically shook his head.

"AA is great. It saved my life! But it's not church. You need Jesus, and you won't find Him here. Some meetings won't even let you refer to Jesus by name when you share. No, you need a church where you can get plugged in to God, not a 'Higher Power.' And you need to find friends who believe in Him too."

"But where? I'm out of ideas."

"I'll tell you what. Why don't you visit the church I've been going to? I'm not a member yet, but I like it. The people are nice, and they serve an amazing potluck. You can meet me there next Saturday."

I nodded, unconvinced but willing to try one more time.

CHAPTER

3

By the end of summer, I was regularly attending Hal's Seventh-day Adventist church in the San Fernando Valley. I knew a little about Adventists from my brother Tom and his wife, Cindy. Her parents left the faith before she was born, so their opinions were not positive. Since faith was never part of my upbringing, I knew that attending any church would bring criticism and teasing from friends and family.

One reason I kept going was the members. They were friendly, sweet, and refreshingly wholesome. At potluck, everyone made me feel welcome—something I hadn't always felt at family barbecues or my friends' parties. So I ignored the naysayers and kept going.

At the same time, my months of sobriety in AA started adding up. Drinking had never been a huge issue because I had always hated my father's alcoholism. He was a mean drunk. Alcohol brought out the worst in him, including verbal and sexual abuse throughout my childhood. The drugs, however, were harder to walk away from. I couldn't be around them without giving in to temptation, so I stopped hanging around friends who still used them, even Julie. Missing old friends was the hardest part of sobriety. Thankfully, I had no qualms about leaving the occult behind. Getting it out of my life was like taking out smelly trash. In its place, I craved a new, fresher kind of life to match what I saw at church.

Despite that yearning, going from being pagan to Adventist was like crossing the Grand Canyon: there was no easy way, and it couldn't be accomplished in a day. The world still held my attention; and I often felt torn, wondering just how much God expected me to give up. I was young. I needed fun and excitement; two things I didn't find much of at church. Since family and old friends usually engaged in the wrong kinds of fun, AA became an oasis of neutrality, where people didn't party, but they didn't judge either. On the contrary, they were all about making sobriety fun with dances and parties.

Meanwhile, as fall unfolded, I realized it was time to be on my own. Adulthood was out there, beyond the confines of the guesthouse and the lake. Breaking those confines required a car. Thankfully, Mom encouraged my sobriety by buying me a vintage Ford Fairlane. Everything got a lot easier.

On a warm Monday morning in September, with a tank full of gas and a heart full of hope, I fired up the engine and headed for the employment office in the valley. I joined fellow job seekers in scouring walls posted with three-by-five-inch index cards that listed jobs, hoping for something basic enough to get my foot in the door—fast.

Pulling off a promising card, I took it to the clerk.

"This is for a home companion. Have you ever taken care of anyone who's sick or elderly?"

Biting my lip, I shook my head.

"This woman has cancer. She'll need you to cook, clean house, and generally just be there for whatever she might need. Do you think you could handle that?"

"I've been cooking and cleaning for my family since I was twelve. I don't mind helping someone who's sick. I'm sure I could do the job if you'll let me try."

The woman tapped her fingers in thought. "This job requires you to drive her to doctors' appointments. How old are you? Do you have a valid driver's license with a clean record?"

"Yes. I'm nineteen."

Her eyebrows shot up. "You don't look it. I thought you might still be in high school. Well, you appear strong and healthy. This says she's thirty-three. She might enjoy having someone your age there. OK, I'll call and let her know you're coming for an interview." She wrote down the address. "If you go now and make a good impression, you can probably start right away." She handed back the card. "Good luck."

I drove straight to the home of Anna Manconi. This was my first job interview. I had no idea what to expect. I nervously rang the doorbell and waited. A TV played somewhere inside. Slow, shuffling footsteps approached. Then a beautiful, nightgown-clad woman slowly opened the heavy wood door. Her chestnut hair was cut in a pageboy style that needed combing. Her dark, almond-shaped eyes were lovely but looked sleepy as they blinked at the sunlight.

"Are you Cheryl?" she asked, swaying slightly. I wondered if she might fall over. Her hand retained a good grip on the door, so I tried not to show undo concern.

"Yes," I said, flashing my best high-school drill-team smile. "I've come for the job."

Stepping aside, Anna let the door swing open wider. With a wobbly gait, she led the way to the living room and gestured me to follow. She turned down the volume on the soap opera and plopped heavily into an upholstered recliner. The drapes were drawn, and the room needed airing.

I was supposed to be there, but I felt like an intruder. I sat gingerly on a straight-backed chair and nervously played with my hair, not sure what was supposed to happen next. "Are you all right?" I finally asked. "You seem unsteady."

"I'm fine, if you don't count the cancer eating up my spine," Anna quipped with a sad smile. At my surprised look, she added, "I just took pain meds. They make me woozy. It will pass."

Anna asked where I lived and why I wanted the job. Then she went over the duties and hours.

"If you still want the job, I think you'll do just fine. But you live with your parents half an hour away. Can you make that drive every day? I can't have you coming late."

"Living with them is temporary. My friend Connie recently had a baby and wants to share a place in North Hollywood, not too far from here. We're already looking. I hope to move soon."

That seemed to satisfy her. I agreed to start the next day.

Getting used to working forty hours a week was a huge adjustment, but I liked Anna, and the work was easy. When she had appointments, we took her 1967 Camaro, the fastest and most fun car I had ever driven. The job was working out.

A month later Connie and I moved into an inexpensive two-bedroom, two-bath apartment, ending my long commute. Living with Connie and her infant daughter, Noel, was a far cry from my solitary existence in the guesthouse. I had to learn how to budget, divide chores, and fill my off hours. Adulthood was an amazing mix of responsibilities and choices. I had no parents or live-in landlords telling me how to live, but church soon presented lifestyle conflicts I hadn't bargained for.

The first was diet. The ladies at the potlucks said they only served vegetarian dishes. It was healthier. If I did eat meat, it should be biblically clean meats such as beef, chicken, or certain fish, never pork or shellfish. I didn't understand. I had eaten all kinds of meats my entire life and had never gotten sick. Yet conviction hit whenever I ate Dad's barbecued spareribs or a slice of bacon; I was worried that I was offending God.

This temptation was even trickier around Anna. I hesitated to tell her about any lifestyle changes until I had firmly made up my own mind on the matter. Then one day something happened that tested my ability to balance my health principles with putting others first and placing humility before pride.

It all started when Anna asked me to dress up a little the next day for her appointment, foregoing my usual jeans, T-shirt, and flip-flops. Unfortunately, in the rush to get to work on time, I forgot my platform sandals and drove to work barefoot.

When it was time to leave for her appointment, Anna looked keenly disappointed. "Where are your shoes?"

I was still wearing the fuzzy pink slippers I kept at her house to clean in. I explained that I had forgotten my shoes and offered to wait in the car while she went inside to buy the makeup she needed.

Anna shook her head. "The salon is in the Beverly Hills Hotel. The hallways are long. I need you for balance when I walk."

"Can't I just go barefoot?"

"The hotel requires shoes. I know you didn't mean to forget, but you'll have to be brave and wear your slippers. Just hold your head high." Then she sweetly added, "At least your outfit is cute."

Looking down, I agreed. My lacy top and wraparound skirt were appropriate for the hotel. But fuzzy pink slippers? I suddenly hated my own chronic lack of organization.

The hotel was beautiful and stately—movie-star glamorous with pink stucco, lush foliage, tall palm trees, and fancy new cars. I pointedly ignored the bemused grins of onlookers and helped Anna complete her errand. Afterward, I anxiously looked forward to escaping to her car. But at the last minute, she suddenly veered left, away from the hotel exit.

"This way, Cheryl," she said, pulling me down another hallway.

Obligated to obey, I escorted her into the famed Polo Lounge. Panic filled me afresh as we traversed the crowded, noisy restaurant. She didn't slow down until we settled in a comfy leather booth. Not far away, a boisterously loud Ed McMahon celebrated with several equally animated friends. Looking around, I spotted more celebs in the posh room. Even though I'd grown up around people in the entertainment industry, I felt like I was a fish out of water.

Anna flashed a happy smile. "Don't you just *love* this place? I ate here all the time when I lived on this side of town."

Seeing her joy, I forgot about the slippers. No one could see them under the table anyway. The important thing was that Anna looked happier than I had ever seen her; her sickness and pain all but forgotten for the moment. She didn't care that we were plain folk among the elite. She was having a great time!

"Have you ever had a Monte Cristo sandwich?" she asked, pointing to the menu. At my headshake, her smile grew. "Oh, you *must* try one. They're delicious! I'll order one for each of us."

The menu described the triple-decker club sandwich as being made with turkey and ham, dipped in batter, deep fried, and then dusted with powdered sugar. I momentarily considered telling her I didn't eat pork. But I didn't have the heart to squelch her enthusiasm or spoil her outing. So we stuffed ourselves on the sweet, savory sandwiches and indulged in some serious people watching while Anna happily told stories of her glory days working as a hospital technician and dating handsome doctors.

Not long after our lunch date, when I was sure of my own decision, I shared with Anna that my diet was changing along with my faith. She understood. By that time, we were friends, and she deserved to know who I was becoming, as I moved from a haphazard diet to one geared toward pleasing God.

As my diet gradually changed, other lifestyle choices cropped up at church that created far larger struggles. Like most people in AA, I had smoked since high school. I didn't want to quit, though it was obvious no one at church smoked. Beyond tobacco, the yearning for romance also proved irresistible. There was no one my age at church to date, only married couples and senior citizens. So I looked elsewhere. Free to do as I pleased, I went to AA dances. Not knowing any better, I followed the social mores of my day, viewing sex as a right of adulthood, not a moral dilemma.

Naturally, over time, those choices clashed with the church. I found myself straddling an uncomfortable spiritual fence, always looking for balance. Sometimes I felt in control. Other times I lay awake at night feeling guilty, wondering where I truly belonged. Life might have gone on like that indefinitely except that a certain, precious consequence came along, demanding a day of reckoning.

* * * * *

"Sit down." Marlene patted the bed, then turned down the volume on the TV. "Read your fourth step." My AA sponsor was in her midforties and nursing a back injury.

For several minutes, I read through a "searching and fearless moral inventory" of myself, one of the Twelve Steps of AA. The purpose was to purge the past by admitting wrongs committed against others and one's self. It was supposed to make me feel free; instead, it felt humiliating and shameful. True to the spirit of AA, Marlene listened without judgement until I finished.

"Good job," she praised, patting my hand. "I know that was hard, but you have more to do. No one gets it all out at once. Your past has many layers. It takes several excavations to reach the bottom."

I nodded as the doorbell rang.

"Come in!" she bellowed. The front door opened, and heavy footsteps approached.

"Alan!" she greeted. A tall man with glasses and a mustache entered the room without hesitation. His curly brown afro was crowned by a flat-topped, brown leather hat with feathers. He wore blue jeans, a flannel shirt revealing a slight tummy, and a quirky smile.

"Hi Marlene," he said, leaning in for a hug. He had an easygoing manner.

"Cheryl, do you know Alan?"

I shook my head shyly.

"I know Marlene from NA [Narcotics Anonymous]. You should try going—it's more fun than AA."

They each chuckled. Both programs use the same Twelve Steps and refer to a "Higher Power" in place of God. But in my mind, NA was for heroin addicts, not me. Alan read my mind.

"I've been clean from heroin for three years. Right, Marlene? Nothing like sobriety!"

"Cheryl was just reading her fourth step. She's one of my new babies." She gave him a firm finger shake. "She's still a newcomer. Don't go getting ideas, Alan."

"You know me better than that, Marlene," he said, sounding wounded. "I just stopped by on my way to Jerry's Deli to pick up dinner." He looked at me. "*Silver Streak* is on cable tonight. I wouldn't mind some company if you like deli food. Strictly casual."

Alan was older and taller than anyone I had ever dated. He was nothing like the blond surfers and football players I had dated in school. But I liked his confident, engaging smile. And I dearly loved deli food.

"OK," I said. "Sounds fun. Marlene, are you coming?"

"Oh, not me! I'm in this bed till my back stops aching. You two go ahead. Just behave yourselves. And remember, no relationships the first year. This is just dinner. Right?"

"Of course, darlin'," he cooed with a wink. "Just a little food and a flick." He gestured for me to get up. "Let's go, I'm starved! See you, Marlene."

Marlene waved us out as she turned the TV's volume back up.

* * * * *

We spent the evening in Alan's 1920s Silver Lake bungalow, sitting on the wood floor in front of his TV with deli food spread out on the coffee table. We had matzo ball soup, corned beef sandwiches on rye, potato salad, and dill pickles. The food was delicious; the movie hilarious; and the company more fun than I had enjoyed in a long time. When he drove me back to Marlene's, he leaned in for a quick kiss.

"I'd like to have dinner again," he said. "In a restaurant next time. How about Saturday?"

"But Marlene said—"

"I know what Marlene said. This is just a date, not a relationship."

I remembered her warnings and wondered where this next date would lead. Alan was great, but he wanted more than a couple of dates. Beyond sobriety, our spiritual paths were far apart. He was Jewish but didn't go to temple. His God was the Higher Power of NA. We could never be like the families at church I so wanted to emulate. He was secular. I called myself a Christian, even though AA meetings far outweighed the time I spent at church. AA was clouding the light of my faith. It was hard to wait for a godly man my own age when this man was right here, asking me out. I knew I should say No, but I didn't.

For several weeks, we saw a lot of each other. We attended meetings and AA dances in Hollywood. He was a great dancer. It was fun. I helped him at the Rose Bowl Flea Market, modeling feather-embellished clothing and jewelry for his small business while he rang up sales. We ate at nice restaurants. And I started sleeping over, something Marlene frowned at but did not forbid.

"Being in a sexual relationship can lead to pain, and pain can lead to a slip," she warned. "You're an adult, so I'm not here to tell you what to do. Just don't drink. Promise me you'll call if he breaks your heart and you need to talk. He's a good man. Who knows? It may turn out all right."

It didn't. In less than two months, I was pregnant. It was winter, and Alan and I were planning a ski trip to Mammoth Lakes. I had to tell him about the baby.

"Can you ski like that?" he asked.

"I guess. I'm not that far along."

Looking down at the slight roundness of my belly, he grew pensive. Finally, he blew out a breath. "Are you going to keep it? I could pay for an abortion if you want."

I shook my head. "No abortion. I don't know if I'll raise it, but I'm definitely going to have it."

"Do you want me to marry you?"

"You're sweet, Alan. I like you a lot. But we both know we're not in love. I don't want to marry you, and I can tell you don't want that either. Thanks for asking though."

Despite everything, we went skiing and had fun. But after the trip, when a friend asked if she could go out with Alan, I realized it was time to face the future on my own. There would be no marriage, but a baby was coming. I had some thinking to do. Where would God fit into this unfolding picture? Was this baby the result of my own self-will run riot or God's plan for my life? I didn't know. I watched Connie and Noel with new interest, seeing how much work single motherhood was. I also saw Connie's joy.

Meanwhile, my church attendance dropped to almost zero. No one there knew about the pregnancy except Hal. He didn't condemn me and merely reiterated how important it was to get right with God and stay that way, not only for my sake but for the coming child as well. Unsure of what lay ahead I kept trudging on, hoping a plan would reveal itself soon.

* * * * *

It was late. I had fallen asleep early and awoke with a start, drenched in sweat. The room was dark, and I couldn't move. I tried to speak, but no words came out. I struggled to speak the name *Jesus*. When it finally came out, loud and clear, the room snapped back to normal. This attack hadn't lasted as long as the ones in the guesthouse, but it was troubling to realize the hiatus I had enjoyed was now inexplicably over. Deep down, I wondered if it was the pregnancy stirring up the enemy. After all, it was wrong to be young, single, and pregnant—not exactly the picture of wholesome Christianity. I knew that. What I didn't know was how to fix it. Peering into the darkness, I wondered who was watching me. Were the demons right there, looking down in mockery at my predicament? Or was it God who looked down? If so, how did He see me? With disappointed anger? Or loving mercy?

I closed my eyes, afraid to pray as hot tears trickled out. The apartment was still, making me drowsy. Suddenly, there was noise and the sounds of anger. It was Connie and her boyfriend, Ben, arguing in her bedroom. Ben had come for dinner and stayed. Their voices rose, then Ben opened Connie's door and stomped down the hall, slamming the front door on his way out. In his wake, Noel started crying.

I lay there, unsure what to do. Then Connie entered my doorway, with her silhouette in shadow. "Sorry about that," she said, sounding tired and sad. She gently rocked a whimpering Noel in her arms. "He gets hot under the collar sometimes."

"His temper scares me. How do you stand it?"

She sighed, pulling her long, black hair to one side and out of Noel's reach. "I don't know. Love, I guess. I need him. He's Noel's father." She sat on the bed so Noel could nurse. Connie, a recovering heroin addict, was pencil thin and seemed fragile. I wondered if she was still sober. "Don't worry; he'll be fine. In fact, he's moving in next weekend. I would have told you before, but you haven't been home much."

"Ben's going to live here? All the time? Connie, he stole money from me just last week!"

Connie stiffened. "He said he'd pay you back. You should know better than to leave cash lying around. He's an ex-addict, after all."

"It wasn't lying around; it was under my lamp. Besides, I don't want to live with a man. Especially one that yells and slams doors."

"Well, I want him here. I already told him he could. So what are you going to do?"

Despite understanding her dilemma, I felt betrayed and shoved aside. But I wasn't trapped. "I'll get my own place. Alan says Silver Lake has lots of inexpensive apartments. I'll find something."

Connie squeezed my hand. "I'm sorry. I didn't mean for things to turn out this way."

I nodded. Nothing was turning out the way either of us had intended.

* * * * *

I found the perfect place: a 1930s Spanish-style bungalow on the side of a hill above Sunset Boulevard. The complex was loaded with bougainvillea, roses, and mature trees that gave ample shade. My bungalow was small; a single room in front for the bed, an eat-in kitchen, bathroom, and a smaller room on the side for clothes and storage. It cost seventy-five dollars a month, which was cheap even for that time. The landlords were a sweet, older couple, and the neighbors looked out for one another.

It was a longer commute to work but close to my mother's campus. I had missed painting, so I signed up for art classes at night, ignoring news reports that the Hillside Strangler was on the prowl in Silver Lake. The demonic attacks were infrequent, but I hadn't gotten used to being alone yet, especially when random noises occurred and shadows lingered and moved in dark corners. It didn't help that sometimes police sirens and gunshots rang out from Sunset Boulevard below.

One night was especially scary. I felt a dark heaviness in the room as a storm raged outside, with howling winds, lightning, and thunder. I lit every lamp, turned up the heat, made hot tea, and got busy on a painting assignment. So far, my paintings were turning out as I wanted, serene and well composed. Settling in front of the easel, I got to work.

Suddenly, there were several loud bangs on the front door. It reminded me of how the demon used to bang on the walls of my parents' house. Frightened, I sat motionless, willing it to stop. Someone or something was out there, and they wanted in! The heavy wood door did not have a peephole or a safety chain. The room's only window faced north, away from the door. There was no way to peek outside to see who was there. After a short respite, the pounding started again, louder this time. Through the wind, I thought I heard a voice shouting but couldn't make out the words or the sex of the person shouting. Finally, I couldn't stand it anymore. I flipped on the porch light and opened the door a crack, bracing my shoulder against it, just in case.

"Yes?" I peered through the crack. With a shaky hand, the person pushed back the coat's hood and moved wet hair out of the way. It was an older, attractive woman, bedraggled and drenched. She looked lost, desperate to get out of the rain. Relief flooded through me as I took in her sad situation. She was not dangerous. I opened the door wider.

"I'm looking for the Thompsons' bungalow. Do you know where they live?"

I pitied the poor creature, nicely dressed under all that rain. But the heaviness I had felt all evening wouldn't allow me to invite her in. I pointed upstairs, and she went back out into the rain. I felt bad, but her loud banging had filled me with dread.

* * * * *

"So what are you going to do?" Anna asked. I was sitting on her living-room floor, folding laundry, watching a commercial for disposable diapers. It was late morning on a warm spring day. I was about halfway through the pregnancy. A decision needed to be made soon.

"My friends think I'd be crazy to raise a child alone. My family either pretends it isn't happening or doesn't talk to me at all, like I died or something. My brother Tom hasn't said a word. Neither has my sister Ellen. Of course, she's all the way in Hawaii; but so what? The only one that stays in touch is my mom, but she won't tell me what to do."

"And Alan? What is he doing to help?"

"Nothing. He said from the beginning this is my deal, not his. Besides, he and my friend are talking marriage. He's out of the picture."

"What about the people at church? What do they have to say about it?"

"I haven't been in a while. Now that I'm showing, I'm embarrassed to go. The only one I've seen from church is Hal, and that's because he helped me buy the '68 Camaro. It's faster than yours."

"I don't know about that," she laughed. "But back to you. No one has any suggestions?"

"My dad offered to pay an attorney to put the baby up for adoption."

"Is that what *you* want?" she asked tenderly.

That was the question of the hour. What *did* I want? Dad's option was logical. After delivering the baby, my life would go on as before. I could finish school, choose a career, find a husband, and start a family with him. Those were all very good things. On the other hand . . .

I stopped folding towels and thought about the mother in the commercial, rocking her freshly diapered baby in a sweet-looking nursery decorated with stuffed animals and fluffy, white curtains. It was an idyllic picture outside my reality. But it made my heart ache anyway. In that moment, I knew.

"I want to keep this baby," I declared with finality, daring to hope. "I can't imagine giving birth and then handing the baby over to someone else to raise. That would kill me."

"Then keep it."

I looked at her, searching for any hint of sarcasm. I found only sincerity. "You really think I can?"

"Cheryl, you can do anything you set your mind to. If raising this baby is what you want, then don't let other people tell you differently. It's your life. You choose."

My heart warmed as her words sunk in and took hold. It would be hard. Nothing about my life would ever be the same again. Everything I did from that point on would affect two people, not just one.

"Everyone says I'm having a boy," I confessed ruefully. "But I want a girl!"

"I think it's a girl. I always have, ever since you told me you were pregnant. Remember?"

I nodded at the memory. "I was so scared to tell you! I thought you'd fire me."

Anna snorted. "Fire you? I can't get along without you! Though I'll have to soon enough."

I rubbed my already-bulging belly.

"Has the doctor said anything about smoking?" she asked gently. "It didn't used to be a big deal, but now reports show that mothers who smoke run a risk of harming their unborn babies."

"I know. I've heard that too. Dr. Ewing keeps bugging me to quit. But it's so hard! Everyone I know, except you, smokes all the time. Every time I try to cut back, I have withdrawals."

"Well, I don't mean to be pushy. I just wondered if you knew."

"You? Pushy?" I laughed with a teasing smile. "Anyway, thanks for the pep talk. It's good to know you're on my side." With some effort, I got up from the floor and picked up the basket of folded towels. "I'm going to go put these away and fix lunch. I'll be back."

Anna smiled with delight and started watching her favorite soap opera. As I walked away, I wondered if she would ever know what a wonderful gift she had given me that day—the courage to follow my own heart. Maternal love flooded my being with the knowledge that I wanted this baby more than I'd ever wanted anything in my life. The only nagging worry left was Hal's warning. Would Satan go after this child?

CHAPTER

4

While shopping for food one late May evening, I stumbled on a magazine article that outlined how to quit smoking with fewer withdrawal symptoms. In the basket it went. That night I studied the plan, not realizing until much later that it was a Seventh-day Adventist magazine. The plan suggested quitting cold turkey—no tapering off—and avoiding places, foods, and other habits linked with smoking, such as drinking coffee in the morning or meeting up with other smokers. They recommended baths twice a day to rid the skin of nicotine coming out of the pores, brisk walks after meals, and hard candy or pickles in between to curb cravings.

I started the following week. Just days into it, Carl called with a surprising invitation. "Hey, my mother wants us to come over for dinner with her new husband Saturday night."

My mind reeled. Carl's mother, Babette, was a wealthy attorney and the second-in-command of the legal department at a major Hollywood studio. Her husband was a Beverly Hills plastic surgeon. Babette's sister was married to a movie star. Their father had amassed a fortune asphalting Los Angeles and building marble-clad skyscrapers. In short, Carl's family made my family look humble. Why would she invite me to her swanky new house in Beverly Hills?

"Carl, I've only met her once—last year before the movie premiere. Remember? She wasn't even married then. I'm sure Babette doesn't remember me. Why would she invite me to dinner?"

Carl chuckled. "Because I asked her to."

I silently weighed his meaning as neighbors walked past my porch and a sparrow eyed me from the lavender tree outside the window.

"Cheryl? Are you still there?"

"Yeah. Just thinking. Does she know I'm pregnant? And that you're *not* the father?"

"Yes. I told her everything. And she really wants you to come. Can you make it?"

Panic hit. I suddenly needed a smoke. I didn't want to hurt his feelings. He sounded so sincere. "Sure," I finally relented. "You'll have to tell me how to get there."

"No way. I'll pick you up so you can't chicken out. Next Saturday at five thirty. Be ready."

I hung up and walked outside for air. Along the way, I noticed my neighbor had his door open. Jack was a talented sculptor who made small, beautiful figures in bronze.

"How's the baby doing?" he called out.

I patted my belly. "Fine. Kicking all the time and growing. How is the ballerina coming along?"

"Come see!" he encouraged, waving me in.

His apartment was larger than mine. He gestured to drawings of ballerinas in various poses.

"I'm leaning toward this one." He pointed to a girl holding toe shoes. "What do you think?"

I studied them all, wishing I had his skill. "This one." Her arms were outstretched. "She looks hopeful."

Jack considered, then shrugged. "Maybe. Hey, you're getting to be a pretty good little painter. Let me know when you're done with the girl's face. I'll pay you one hundred and fifty dollars for it."

"Jack, it's only an assignment."

"I know. Like I said, you're good."

I smiled. "OK. I'll let you know. Well listen, I really need a walk. See you."

"Stay safe out there."

Out on the tree-lined street, I barely noticed the spring flowers in every yard. My mind was focused on Carl. Why did he want Babette to know me better? And why did I say Yes?

* * * * *

Carl arrived wearing jeans and a T-shirt with a picture of the rock band his mom also represented. I wore a pretty cotton dress that felt more like a tent than summer chic. We drove down Sunset Boulevard toward the University of California, Los Angeles.

"Do you like your new stepdad?" I asked nervously.

"Better than the last one. Stan's OK. Seems nice enough."

I couldn't help but notice the stately homes and fancy cars we passed. "Must be nice," I mused, pointing to an old Spanish-style mansion set back from the road.

"Money doesn't make you happy," Carl quipped. "My family is loaded with it, and most of them aren't happy. But I wouldn't mind having a better car." He laughed, giving the dusty dashboard a thump.

Along the way, we reminisced about our exploits while exploring parts of Hollywood where we had no business going, such as the tops of bank buildings and the super-secret Scientology headquarters.

"We had fun, didn't we?" he asked, then turned the car up a narrow, twisting road. He parked in a brick-paved driveway in front of a fancy ranch house, which was surrounded by meticulously trimmed shrubbery and trees. Soft lighting emanated from a large bay window that was framed by drapes.

"This is it? It's smaller than her last house. Pretty though."

"It's big enough for the two of them." He looked at me expectantly. "Ready?"

I swallowed hard. I would never be ready. But we couldn't stay in the car all night. "Ready as I'll ever be."

Brick steps led to a porch decorated with fern-filled urns and a wrought-iron bench. Carl rang the doorbell and stepped back. The door opened, letting us hear the soft classical music playing inside.

"Welcome!" A handsome middle-aged man greeted us. His clothes were elegantly casual, in sharp contrast to ours. "Carl," Stan said, shaking Carl's hand.

"Stan," Carl replied politely.

"And you must be Cheryl." Stan kept his gaze discreetly above my distended belly. "Come in! We're so glad you came. Babette," he called over his shoulder. "The kids are here. Come say hello."

Babette emerged from the kitchen, wiping her hands on a pretty, white apron. She gave her son a brief hug, then placed her hands gently on my arms. "Cheryl, thank you for coming. Why don't you come with me to the kitchen while I finish making the salad? The boys can talk in the living room. You don't mind, do you, Carl?"

At his shrug, Babette led the way to a warm, modern kitchen that showed clear evidence of her culinary efforts. Pots, pans, spoons, and spices covered the countertop and stove in disarray. Babette was in her element. The room smelled heavenly, stirring my appetite and dispelling my nervousness as she put me to work slicing an avocado.

"So what are you up to these days? Carl tells me you're studying art at

Los Angeles City College. What kind of art are you pursuing?"

"Drawing and oil painting this semester. I haven't figured out yet what kind of work I want to get into; my mom is pushing for tech theater or set design. I'm just learning the basics for now."

Babette nodded encouragingly while pulling a small roast from the oven. "A woman needs job skills," she said with friendly conviction. "You never know when you might need them."

Laying a hand on my belly, I nodded. "I also take care of a woman with cancer. What I really want is a career, not just a job. Your career sounds awesome. Carl told me about the studio. That's cool."

For the next few minutes, we chatted while she carved the roast, and I filled large bowls with side dishes. Babette told me more about her job at the studio and the challenges of decorating a new house. When everything was ready, we moved the food to the dining table and called Stan and Carl to join us. The evening passed in easy conversation as we ate. Babette and Stan were perfect hosts, putting Carl and me at ease. But I still wondered why I was there.

We had sorbet for dessert, then Stan and Carl vanished while Babette and I cleaned up.

"Here, let me," she said, taking a stack of dishes from me. "You shouldn't carry anything heavy."

I blushed at her reference to my condition. I was used to doing my share of the housework, but she was right. My back was throbbing, and my balance dubious.

"Thanks," I said.

"I'll finish clearing the table. Why don't you wrap up the meat?" She moved with swift efficiency to rinse dishes and load the dishwasher while I put away leftovers. When there was nothing left to clean up, she turned knowing eyes in my direction and smiled gently. "What do you plan to do after the baby comes? Will you keep your apartment or move back home with your parents? And what about school? It would be a shame to quit."

I swallowed hard at her reasonable questions. I should have answers to them. "I don't know," I admitted. "I don't want to live with my folks. But it will be hard raising a baby alone." Unexpected tears sprang from nowhere. I blinked them away. "Sorry; hormones." I reached for a tissue. "I hope to continue school, but I don't exactly have a plan yet."

She gave me a quick hug, then got busy tidying up the already neat kitchen. "I didn't mean to pry, dear. I just wondered how you're going to get along. You know I raised my three boys alone for the most part and had to rely on babysitters while I finished law school. So I know better than most what a hard road you have ahead. Well, we'd better join the boys before they start feeling neglected."

When the evening was over, Carl and I rode in near silence back to my apartment. A plan, Babette had said. I needed a plan. At the moment, my only plan was to eat a pickle as soon as I got home to stave off cravings.

Carl parked near the entrance to my apartment complex. "You're awfully quiet. What's on your mind?"

I looked at the city lights all around us, which dotted the hillsides and beyond. "Your mom asked what my plans are once the baby comes."

"And?"

"I told her I have no plan. I've been so busy working and finishing school projects that I haven't had time to think about the future. But she's right; I need to figure things out."

Reaching across the car, Carl rested his hand on mine. "I have an idea," he ventured.

I looked at him nervously, wondering where this was going. "Like what? Go back to Alan? He's marrying someone else. Move in with my parents? No thanks." A frustrated sigh escaped as I closed my eyes and pulled back my hand. Instead of letting go, he held on more firmly.

"Actually, I thought you might marry me."

My eyes flew open to meet his. Dinner at his mother's house suddenly made perfect sense. His gaze never wavered. He meant business.

"Carl, we aren't even dating! You're one of my best friends, but that's it. We're just friends. You *know* that."

"I know that's how *you* feel. But I do love you, Cheryl. A lot. I've tried to tell you before, but you always change the subject."

I needed the right words to let him down gently. I did not want to hurt him. "Carl, you know I love you as a friend, but it wouldn't be right to marry you without being *in* love with you."

He set his jaw stubbornly and leaned closer. "You could learn to love me, Cheryl. And my family is rich, *very* rich. I could take care of you and the baby. My mother thinks you're adorable. Even Stan approves. He said so tonight." At my headshake, he pushed on. "I would love your baby as if it were my own. Please marry me. Let me take care of you!"

I met his pleading eyes, then slowly pulled my hand away. "I can't believe you're trying to do such a grand, wonderful thing for me and this child that I'm carrying. But the answer is *No*. I won't marry you just to have a plan." Pain filled his features. "I'm sorry, Carl. I don't mean to hurt you. I just can't do that to you—to us. You deserve better than that."

He turned away, hiding his face in the shadows. "You're wrong. I deserve to be with the girl I love. But I won't keep you here, arguing about it all night. It's late. I'll walk you to the door."

Days later, Carl called with new plans. "I quit my job today. I'm moving to Idaho in two weeks."

"What? It's because of me, isn't it? You're leaving because I won't marry you."

He sighed. "Partly. I'm also sick of Los Angeles. Idaho is beautiful and uncrowded. Besides, my dad lives there. I want to get to know him better." He paused, then added, "I'll see you before I go."

We met once for coffee, then my best buddy, my partner in crime, was gone. I still had no plan.

* * * * *

It was now June. The baby was due in September—not much time to get ready. Just getting through each day was hard, especially without air conditioning. The toughest task was carrying groceries up and down the stairs outside. I had already fallen once, spilling groceries everywhere. What if that happened when I was carrying the baby? Parking was scarce too; one more difficulty that would increase with a baby. In short, I was beginning to wonder if my perfect little home would be perfect for more than just me. Then out of the blue, Beth had an idea.

I met her for lunch at Follow Your Heart, a popular health-food market with a tiny restaurant. It always drew a mix of movie stars and hippies. We ordered veggie sandwiches piled high with alfalfa sprouts.

Beth took a long drink of iced tea and looked at me intently. "I've been thinking," she said. "We should move in together."

I blinked in surprise. "Why? You love your place. And I'm OK where I'm at, sort of."

"No, you're not. Listen, I'm your best friend and I won't let you go through this alone! You can't have a baby by yourself! Especially out in Silver Lake, away from everyone. What if something goes wrong? How would anyone get to you in time? It's ridiculous."

I hated the idea of giving up my own space. Still, Beth made sense; it would be good to have someone right in the next room to help.

"Also, since Alan isn't in the picture, I'd like to be your Lamaze coach. You need one."

I chuckled. "You've been giving this baby thing some thought! You'd have to take classes with me. You up for that?"

"Why not? I've already looked into it. They're free at the community center. They meet once a week. Besides, seeing a baby being born would be cool."

"OK. Thanks, Beth. It would be great to have you in there with me. But I don't know about moving in together."

"Well, start thinking about it. Remember, you live thirty minutes away from your doctor, the hospital, and me. Even if nothing goes wrong, you'd still have to drive yourself to the hospital once you go into labor. That doesn't sound smart to me. We could find something cheap right here in the valley."

I knew she was right. "I'll think about it. Hey, are you going to eat all your chips? I'm starved!"

Beth laughed and slid them over to me. "Here you go, little mommy."

* * * * *

By July, the decision was made. Beth and I moved into a large two-bedroom apartment in Reseda. It was an upstairs unit but only one flight. The rent was cheap, and it had air conditioning in the living room. Best of all, we lived just five minutes from the hospital. Even the Lamaze classes were going well; my life was headed in a more purposeful direction.

The one thing missing was church. It had been months since I had attended, as I was still afraid of what others would say. Then one Sabbath near the end of summer, I couldn't wait any longer. I needed God. I got there a little late and slipped into a back pew, trying not to be noticed. After the final song, I walked out to the vestibule, and there was Hal, chatting with an older woman with short, reddish-brown hair showing just a hint of gray. He caught my eye and waved me over.

"Cheryl, this is Pat. She's the church's head deaconess. Pat, this is my friend Cheryl. She's been coming here off and on as a visitor this past year. I thought you could introduce her to some of the ladies. As you can see, she's going to have a baby. I think she could use some wise women in her life."

I blushed at Hal's no-nonsense, straightforward summation. It was all out in the open now!

I shook Pat's outstretched hand. "Hi. Nice to meet you."

"Hi," Pat said. Her eyes were warm with kindness. "Why don't you come with me? The ladies are preparing potluck. I'm sure we can find something for you to do."

Hal smiled. Mission accomplished.

"Hey everyone," Pat called out to the ladies in the large kitchen. "This is Cheryl. She's new to our church and wants to help out. Who has a job for her?"

A robust, sweet-looking older woman with blue eyes and curly, red hair came over immediately. "Hi Cheryl, I'm Gayle. You can help me fill the bread baskets." I followed her to the counter where bags of bread were stacked. "I see you're expecting. When are you due?"

"In September."

"Wow, just around the corner!" She opened a bag of bread and pulled out several slices. "Here, just arrange them like this." She quickly demonstrated. "When you're done, put the baskets out there in the hall with a big tub of margarine on each serving table." She watched me work, then asked, "Is your husband here too?"

There it was, the big question. I shook my head, preparing myself for rejection and judgment. "I'm not married; don't even have a boyfriend."

Gayle looked surprised, but her expression never lost its kindness. "Oh, that's too bad, dear. But never you mind. I'm sure everything will work out fine! Now, I'm going to go check the casseroles. When you're done, we'll tackle the pies. Everyone loves pie!"

I blinked at her for a moment. The rebuff hadn't come. Why? I didn't understand Christian kindness yet. This was my first introduction to belonging to the family of God.

"OK," I said. "I'll be done in a jiffy."

As we moved from one job to the next, Gayle told me about her husband, Jim. She had been a member for years, but he had only recently started attending. She pointed through the door at an older, heavyset man who was helping to set up the tables where people would eat. "He's a shy one, but he's making friends. You will too. You'll see."

With that, the worst was over. I had been taken into the fold without so much as a raised eyebrow. From then on, I attended most Sabbaths, in addition to extra activities, such as game night, the annual talent show, and a prophetic series on end-time events. I was beginning to make a home there.

On the last night of the series, I approached Gayle, who had brought Jim to help him better understand Seventh-day Adventist beliefs. "Gayle, is that really how the world will be someday? It sounds so scary!"

"Most of Revelation is scary. But God will see us through. That's the best part. In the end, when everything is finished, Jesus will be victorious, and Satan will be cast out forever. Then we get to live with God in heaven."

"You make it all sound simple. But I can't take it in. It's too much to understand all at once."

"You could sign up for Bible study with one of the pastors. That would help you understand."

I chuckled. "I do have questions, but now isn't a good time. Maybe after the baby is born."

The days passed slowly as the due date edged closer. I had given up my job working for Anna by then, so money was tight, very tight. To compensate, I ate less meat and filled up on bread and peanut butter, pasta and eggs, cereal and milk, and used the money I saved to buy baby bottles and other small items I would soon need.

I also read the Bible more, and Satan bothered me less. It had been a crazy decision to get baptized with Beth, but I could see it had been a turning point in my relationship with God. He seemed to be taking it seriously, even if I hadn't. In fact, things were going so well that I almost forgot Hal's warning of what Satan might someday do to my child. I didn't realize that Satan was merely biding his time.

CHAPTER

5

By August, finances were tight, and I was bored. I had heard from a friend that a trendy bakery in West Los Angeles was hiring and went to check it out. The gruff owner was dubious that a young mother-to-be would make for a good employee. Even so, after a quick tour he put me to the test by having me make an upright football out of a sheet cake. I succeeded and was promised the job as soon as the baby came.

Meanwhile, the due date was close, and I still needed many things. It was overwhelming, especially since my parents weren't helping. Then one day Mom called out of the blue to ask if she could stop by. When she arrived, I showed her the apartment and the used crib I had purchased from Goodwill. I had cleaned it up and tightened the screws for safety.

"This isn't a bad crib," she said. "The wood is sturdy, and the white paint isn't peeling. But you'll need something to make it more comfortable. Why don't we go shopping and see what we can find?"

Happy for her support, we went to a nearby baby boutique and picked out a mattress liner, sheets, and a matching comforter. My baby had a bed! We chose several other smaller items, and then she surprised me and bought a child's rocker with frilly cushions. What a day!

Back at the apartment, we sat down to drink iced tea.

"I've decided to pay for a diaper service," she announced, then held up a hand at my shocked expression. "Disposables are too expensive. Cloth are much better for the baby's skin. But they're too much work when you don't have a washer and dryer, so a diaper service is the only answer."

"Thanks, Mom," I said sincerely. "That will help a lot. And thanks for everything you got today."

She smiled wistfully. "I wanted to do *something*. I still don't approve of your situation, but the choice wasn't mine to make. Besides, I'm starting to get excited about being a grandmother. I know, Tom and Cindy just had a baby last spring, but they live too far away for me to see him. You're right here. I can enjoy this grandchild."

"What about Dad? Is he still mad that I'm keeping the baby?"

"He's being pretty stubborn about it. Thinks you're throwing your life away." At my sad expression, she squared her shoulders and smiled. "Don't worry; he'll come around. He really just wants the best for you. I don't know why it's so hard for him to show it. Anyway, he can't ignore the fact that you're carrying his grandchild." She got up. "By the way, don't make plans for Friday. I'm taking you for a drive."

"Where? What for?"

"I'll tell you more on Friday. See you then."

* * * * *

On Friday morning, Mom arrived early. We drove to La Verne, a small community east of Los Angeles. She said she had recently joined the board at the University of La Verne and wanted to show me the campus.

"As my daughter, you can attend for free. They have a terrific art program; and just a block from campus, the university has a day care facility that takes newborns. Isn't that wonderful?"

I tried to take in this amazing opportunity that was offered on a silver platter. "Yes; but Mom, it's so far away! Beth and I just moved in together. I have a job waiting for me. And what about church? I could never make that trip every week."

She looked at me with understanding. "I know. It means another big change. But think Cheryl, you could finish your art degree and not have to worry about the baby being taken care of! I've already looked into housing. There are rooms for rent within walking distance of the campus. Come on; let's go see."

She was right. The day care was clean and bright and had a warm, friendly staff. The art building was impressive, with tons of space and light for students to work. Surrounded by pretty houses on tree-lined streets, the campus was beautiful and idyllic. It was also very far from everything familiar and safe.

That night I lay in bed with images of church, the bakery, and the campus swirling in my head. The weeks and months ahead stretched out like a crooked road map, all jumbled and unsure. I didn't know which path to choose. None felt clearly right. Unable to think, I turned off the light to sleep.

Hours later I awoke and found myself paralyzed. The room felt weird. It was a struggle, but as soon as I spoke the name of Jesus aloud, I snapped out of the paralysis immediately. From my bed, I could hear random noises in the next room and went to investigate. Beth's door was shut, and her room quiet. I walked through the moonlit apartment to the kitchen. There was no intruder, and nothing amiss. The noises had stopped, yet the sense of evil clung to me. I shook off my fear and returned to bed to read the Bible.

It was soothing, but my mind kept revisiting all the opposing crossroads that lay ahead, including Carl's marriage proposal. Would any bring back friends and family? What about God? Did He care which road I chose? Maybe accepting Mom's offer would keep her on my side and restore Dad's approval. But what about the ladies at church? Besides Beth and Anna, whom I still saw from time to time, they were the only ones who were consistently kind. I hated the idea of losing their support. The bakery job was not pivotal, but it would pay the bills. Besides, I had given my word. As sleep slowly reclaimed my body, I made the decision that school was too much right now. Classes would be starting right when the baby was due. Perhaps next year, when the baby was older. With the decision made, I fell asleep.

* * * * *

The phone rang. It was Pat, and she wanted to stop by. She soon arrived with big bags of clothes.

"What's that?" I asked while moving out of the way.

"Just some baby things I thought you could use," she smiled. "There's more in the car."

A young girl carrying an umbrella stroller followed her inside. The girl was slender, almost as tall as Pat, and had long, light-brown hair and sweet blue eyes.

"Cheryl, this is my daughter Tracy."

"Hi," Tracy said shyly. "This is for you."

"Thank you," I said, taking the stroller. "Nice to meet you."

"Tracy, let's go get the rest of it. Cheryl, can you hold the screen door for us?"

When they finished unloading, the room looked like a thrift store. The bags contained gender-neutral onesies, sleepers, bibs, T-shirts, booties, receiving blankets, and washcloths. Pat had also brought baby bottles, canned formula, and infant cereal. This baby would not go naked or hungry.

"This is wonderful, Pat. Where did you get it all?"

"Oh, people from church donated what they weren't using anymore. And stores always give the church formula that's about to expire. It will all stay good for months, so don't worry. It's fine."

As I refolded everything, Pat explained there would be more. "In two weeks, the church ladies are throwing you a baby shower for whatever else you need."

"I don't even know most of them! Why would they do such a thing?"

"Because they know you," she said kindly. "They want to help. They want you to know that you and your baby are welcome and wanted at our church."

"After the baby comes," Tracy piped up, "I can babysit. I love babies!"

"That sounds great, Tracy," I said while trying not to cry. "You'll make a terrific babysitter."

The love and generosity coming from virtual strangers was overwhelming. "I don't deserve all this, Pat," I whispered. "Please tell everyone I said thank you."

The shower took place at the senior pastor's home. The house overflowed with women, children, and piles of brightly wrapped presents that included several new baby items, a homemade baby blanket, and a set of Bible Story books. Opening all the presents and listening to the women's comments and questions about each gift wrapped me in love like a huge blanket of my own.

Not to be outdone, Beth gave me a combination birthday and baby shower at our apartment when I turned twenty, with our closest male and female AA friends. Like before, the living room quickly filled up with more practical baby items, plus a three-foot-tall stuffed Wile E. Coyote from Beth's boyfriend Paul, who was the son of a famous television producer. My friends' unpretentious love and acceptance was different from the ladies at church but equally sincere. They were behind me. I was not in this alone.

* * * * *

"Morning," Beth greeted. "It's going to be another hot one."

She wore the long, baggy T-shirt she had slept in. I munched cereal from the box without much interest. Even with the air conditioner running, the apartment was uncomfortably warm. It was mid-September, and I was past my due date. I had only gained eighteen pounds so far; but my belly was so enormous that friends said I looked like a watermelon on a Popsicle stick. All I wanted was cool air and this baby *out*.

"Still nothing?" she asked, glancing at my tummy.

"No, just Braxton-Hicks contractions. I've been having those for a month. There has to be *something* I can do to get things going!"

"I wouldn't know," she quipped. "I've never had a baby."

"Well, if you don't mind, I'm going to ride your bike around the block and give this kid the hint that it's time to get a move on."

It was fun pedaling around the neighborhood, waving at curious on-lookers; but the only thing it did was make me hot and tired. I came home more uncomfortable than ever.

For a week, I tried everything I could think of to bring on labor: long walks, dancing, even jumping jacks. Nothing worked. Like the heat wave, this baby planned to stay put a while longer. Just when I thought I couldn't stand another minute, Mom called.

"Since your father is in China, I thought you might enjoy staying with me to escape the heat."

I agreed. The lake was only twenty miles away but felt deliciously cooler thanks to an ocean breeze. Laura, a friend I had grown up with at the lake, was renting the guesthouse, so I stayed in the main house. For days, I lolled around the house, reading and taking walks around the lake.

Then early one day, that peaceful interlude ended. I had just fixed a bowl of Grape-Nuts and sat down to eat it on the sundeck. The view outside was clear all the way to the lake, but right away I noticed a weird, sour scent in the air. I stood there chewing, wondering what could be wrong. Nothing felt right. I took another bite and chewed, then bit down on a large, bitter chunk of something hard. I looked down. There were cinders floating in the milk. Looking around, I saw only blue sky. Finally, I turned to face the house and the mountain north of it. There, thick, menacing smoke filled the sky. Cinders were raining down from a massive fire racing toward us.

I immediately ran inside to the kitchen where Mom was fixing a roast for dinner that night. Her smile faded when she saw the fear on my face. "What's wrong? Are you in labor?"

"No! There's a fire coming straight for us!"

She dropped what she was doing and followed me outside. One look at the sky said it all.

"Quick, back inside! I'll turn on the roof sprinklers and see if Bret knows anything. Start packing, just in case." Bret was a fire captain who lived next door. She returned minutes later, more worried than before.

"Bret's not home, but there's a fire crew at the bottom of our hill. They said it's out of control and we have to leave. I'll get the important papers. You put your dad's new VCR [videocassette recorder] and camera in the car."

"The VCR? Why?"

"Because it cost a fortune. He'd kill me if I let it burn up in a fire." She ran trembling fingers through her hair. "Stop asking questions, and do what I say. There's no time now to talk!"

The VCR and camera were heavy. I struggled to get them down the hill and into my car. Suddenly, a young firefighter rushed over to help while ash fell around us like snow. He looked scared.

"How close is it?" I asked.

"Very. All the roads to the lake are closed except Kanan, and the flames are jumping that road too. The fire will be here soon. You have to leave."

My heart leapt to my throat. "If the flames are crossing Kanan, how do we get out?"

He swiped an arm across his sweaty, worried brow. "You'll have to take Kanan to the Pacific Coast Highway. It's the only way. Listen, if you encounter a wall of flames, just drive straight through it. Don't stop! You don't want your car overrun with fire. And whatever you do, don't leave the vehicle. Got it?"

I rushed back up to the house. Mom was stuffing papers in a bag.

"Mom, a fireman said we may have to drive through flames to get out. I'm scared!"

Her hands froze midair. "In that case, we'd better take the same car. Come on, let's get what we can into the van."

The VCR was moved one more time, along with paintings and other precious items. It was mind numbing to decide in minutes what possessions were most important and which ones could be left behind. When we drove away, we passed a dozen firefighters watering down our hill, defending our property. I felt like crying but was too frozen with fear to give in to tears.

We drove quickly around the lake to Kanan Road, then south to the ocean, encountering smoke, ash, and flames on either side of the canyon. Road conditions and other cars made traveling slow at times, but we never stopped. Thankfully, no walls of flames blocked our way. When the ocean got close enough to see, the smoke cleared somewhat.

"I think the worst is behind us," Mom said with relief.

We spent the night at my aunt Betty and uncle Winn's house in the valley, watching the news to see how bad the fire was and when we could go home. Since I didn't have my car, it never occurred to me to go back to the apartment. Besides, I was curious to see the condition of our lake community.

The next day we drove back, stopping once at a roadblock to show our residential identification. No one else was allowed in. We saw dozens of firefighters still fighting hot spots. The sky was still smoky, and the air acrid. All around us were blackened hillsides, trees reduced to charred, black stumps, and several homes burned to the ground. The fire burned all the way to the ocean, incinerating people, pets, and possessions along its path. It was an awful, heartbreaking mess.

"We were lucky," Mom said. "Well, let's get all this stuff back into the house. I need a nap."

Mom figured it was sheer chance that our family home still stood. I later learned that several residents who believed in the occult and supernatural powers had united in reaching out to the universe, calling on spirits to keep the lake safe. I chose to believe God had spared our home and our lives, but it bothered me that so many others had not been spared. What had they done, if anything, to deserve total destruction? Was God indiscriminately merciful to some and not to others? I didn't know.

CHAPTER

6

*V*ery early on the Sunday after the fire, while the house was co-cooned in darkness, a cramp made me stir. At first, it felt like more false labor. Then a sharper cramp followed. Over the next hour, they came stronger and closer together. It was time to wake Mom.

I gently nudged her shoulder. "It's time."

Startled awake, she quickly sat up. "How close are they?"

"About fifteen minutes. They're getting stronger."

She slid on a robe. "Let's go to the kitchen and see what happens."

I sat at the kitchen table sipping orange juice. If this *was* labor, food was off limits. Mom made herself coffee and an egg and then pulled out a messy kitchen drawer to organize. "I've been meaning to do this for months," she said before biting the egg. "As good a time as any."

I pulled recipes from the pile to keep my mind off the pain. After an hour, we knew it was time to call Dr. Ewing and go. It was a clear, beautiful day; a good day to give birth.

Beth met us at the hospital, breathless and full of nervous excitement. I was placed in a large, open labor room with other beds that remained empty. Mom stayed in the waiting room while Beth donned a smock and stayed close, watching everything the nurse did. I let the nurse know I wanted an all-natural childbirth, which meant no epidural or pain meds. She looked skeptical but complied.

A large TV high on the wall was tuned to reruns of old *Little Rascals* movies. Slowly, the morning passed by. Around noon, the pain got unbearable. Beth got the nurse.

"I need *something!*" I yelled.

The nurse gave me an I-told-you-so look and peeked under the gown. "It's too late for an epidural. I'll give you a shot of Demerol." She administered it and then went to tell the doctor.

Soon she wheeled me to the delivery room, with Beth following. I felt my small body ripping and tearing. I screamed loudly, then opened my mouth to let out another yell. The nurse looked at me sternly and crammed a washcloth in my mouth to silence me. In the delivery room, the doctor and nurses descended like an army with drapes and instruments.

"Get that thing out of her mouth," Dr. Ewing barked. He adjusted a large mirror above the bed and gave me a masked smile. "Are you ready? Let's get this baby out!"

Everything became a haze of pain and activity. Beth held my hand through each contraction and push, modeling the Lamaze breathing we had learned. Dr. Ewing and the nurses exchanged rapid-fire orders to one another as the birth progressed.

"OK," Dr. Ewing urged. "One more big one. That's it. There's the head. Look up at the mirror so you can see!"

I took one look and turned away, unable to bear the sight. I was in agony and wanted it to be over. I pushed again and felt the baby slide out, then heard a loud cry.

"It's a girl!" he said. "Eight pounds, eleven ounces. Very impressive for such a small mommy."

I fell back exhausted and awed that such a large baby had come out of me. Beth smiled radiantly. "You did it! You have your girl."

I nodded and waited for a nurse to bring her to me. It never happened. Instead, they whisked her away without ever giving me a look. Meanwhile, the doctor got busy sewing me up with more than a hundred stitches. I had torn badly and lost blood. The recovery room was next and hours of waiting.

When the nurse finally decided I was ready, she rolled me down a long hallway to a regular room, where Mom caught up with me.

"Have you seen her? She's beautiful!"

"No, they wouldn't let me. Is she OK?"

"Your baby is fine," the nurse said as she straightened my pillow. "I'll bring her to you soon."

As soon as she came in, I could see that Rachel was indeed beautiful and perfectly formed. I tried cuddling her, but she immediately started crying.

"Did I do something wrong?"

"She's probably just hungry," the nurse said. "Here, I'll show you how to nurse her."

Like all new things, it felt awkward at first. Rachel seemed as unsure as I did. But we got there. When she was done, the nurse demonstrated how to burp her. After that, Rachel looked peaceful for a few moments and then started crying again. The nurse took her.

"I'll take her back to the nursery so you can rest," she said. "Then I'll bring you a light supper."

I watched them go, feeling overwhelmed. Giving birth had been so much harder than anything I had imagined. My body felt unexpectedly empty. And even while she had nursed, I felt strangely disconnected from her. When was bonding supposed to happen? Had I missed the opportunity when they didn't let me hold her at birth? I couldn't picture what caring for a newborn would be like. I so wanted to be a good mother and for my baby to be happy.

"Where's Beth?" I asked Mom, who had stayed to visit.

"Home. She was tired. She'll be back tomorrow. The doctor explained how badly you tore; I'm so sorry. You'll have to stay at least three days to heal up and get your strength back."

"You look tired too," I said. "Go home, and get some rest."

She nodded. "I am beat. It's been a long day. I'll try to visit again before you check out, but your dad flies in tomorrow, so there may not be time. I'll call to let you know."

I wanted to argue that it shouldn't make a difference. In fact, they should both be coming together. Instead, I nodded and said nothing.

*   *   *   *   *

Late that evening I fed Rachel again, then the nurse turned off the bed light. "She'll stay in the nursery for the rest of the night. Try to sleep. You need it."

She was right. I was still exhausted, in pain, and knew that once I left the hospital there would be no one to help with night feedings. I quickly fell asleep and started dreaming. I could see the hospital corridor outside the room. It was a strange mix of light and dark and had a sinister appearance. From down the hall, a baby's cries echoed with misery and desperation. It had to be Rachel. Suddenly, the crying stopped. Panicked voices and urgent whispers of nurses rose as they rushed to and fro out of sight. Something was terribly wrong. Why weren't they coming to tell me? Had something happened to her? Was she dead? I started to cry. I tried to get out of bed to find out for myself, but a dark presence held me down. Then I knew. Satan had done something to her after all, and I couldn't save her.

The next instant I was startled awake by my own cries. I leaned up far enough to see the corridor outside the half-open door. No baby was crying. Everything looked normal. I watched a young nurse come around the corner, then through my door.

"You're awake," she said.

I lay back down, eyeing her cautiously. "Is my baby all right?"

"Of course, why wouldn't she be?"

"No reason," I admitted, realizing I must have been dreaming. But it felt so real. "Can you bring her to me?" I needed to make sure.

"Oh no, the babies are sleeping. We just gave them all a bottle. A nurse will bring her in a few hours, after you've had more sleep and breakfast. Can I get you anything now? Maybe another blanket? It feels chilly in here."

"No, I'm fine," I said without conviction.

After she left, I lay in the dark for a long time, mentally going over the dream. It lingered, still fresh, as a heavy foreboding of darker things to come.

* * * * *

By that afternoon, I felt strong enough to eat a good lunch and sit up, though everything from the navel on down throbbed with pain. Bored with the TV, I turned it off and reached for the phone.

Anna's mother answered, sounding strained.

"It's Cheryl. Is Anna there? I have some news for her."

"Oh," she answered and then paused. Her prolonged silence said something was very wrong.

"Cheryl, I'm sorry to tell you this, but we buried Anna Marie today. She died last week. I would have let you know before, but I couldn't find your number. It's been a difficult time for all of us."

Tears filled my eyes. Anna—my champion cheerleader and most loyal supporter throughout the pregnancy—was gone. She would never see Rachel.

"I'm sorry," I choked out. "I wouldn't have bothered you if I'd known. I . . . I just wanted to tell her that I had a girl. You see, I really wanted a girl, and Anna was the only one who thought all along that it *was* a girl. I wanted so much to bring Rachel to see her."

"Of course, you did. She would have loved that." Another long pause. "Well, I really must go. I have a house full of people to attend. Congratulations, dear, I am happy for you. Anna would be, too, if she was still with us."

Grief flooded me like a river. It took effort to remember there was still much to be thankful for; Anna would have agreed. So when the nurse came in later, I offered a brave smile.

"How are you doing this afternoon?" she asked brightly. "Can I get you anything?"

"I'm fine," I said softly. "I don't need a thing."

* * * * *

Two days later, Beth arrived to take us home. "Where is she? Are you almost ready?"

"Hold on," I laughed. "Help me finish getting dressed first. The doctor is signing the release papers now, and then a nurse will bring Rachel so we can go."

The doctor came to explain how to care for my stitches and what foods to avoid while breastfeeding. "Your daughter is pretty healthy," he said. "Her weight and size are excellent, but she's jaundiced. You'll have to monitor that. Let me know if it gets worse."

"Jaundiced? What's that?"

"Nothing to be alarmed about. It's pretty common in newborns. It should clear up in a few days as she gets stronger. Just let me know if her skin is still yellowish a week from now."

When everything was ready, Beth took the overnight bag and personal items down to the car. The pink onesie and booties for Rachel were laid out on the bed, along with a new receiving blanket.

One of the older nurses entered, carrying the baby in her confident arms. Rachel was placid, not making a sound. "Here she is," the nurse cooed, "all ready to go."

She laid Rachel on the bed, so I could dress her. I hesitantly removed the hospital blanket and checked to see if her diaper was dry.

The nurse chuckled. "Oh, no worries! I just fed and changed her. She's all set for the trip home."

Satisfied, I clumsily maneuvered her wriggling arms and legs into the onesie and closed all the snaps. Then I laid her on the blanket and wrapped it loosely around her.

"Here, let me show you," the nurse said, leaning in. "Babies like it when their blankets are wrapped tightly around them. Makes them feel safe and secure. Like this." She expertly pulled the blanket's corners in snugly. "See?"

Rachel looked like a blanket sausage. "Does it have to be that tight?"

"Yep, see how content she is? Trust me, she likes it. Now I'll go get the wheelchair."

As soon as I was in the wheelchair, the nurse put Rachel in my arms. All went well at first, then Rachel fixed her still dark-blue eyes on my hazel ones and started wailing, then shrieking. I looked at the nurse in a panic, but she merely shrugged unconcernedly.

Blood rushed to my face from embarrassment that I couldn't get my own baby to settle down and stop crying. Beth likewise looked mortified. She was no more equipped to cope with this infant's outburst than I was. Taking my purse, Beth walked silently beside the wheelchair as the nurse pushed it down the long, long corridor, into the crowded elevator of onlookers, down to the lower level, and out the front entrance to the warm outdoors where her cries mercifully had less punch.

The nurse briefly held her while Beth opened the car door and helped me inside, then handed Rachel back with a quizzical look.

"That's the first time I've ever seen *that* happen. Well, good luck!" Then she was gone.

I steeled myself for a noisy ride home; but the second Beth closed the door, Rachel took a shuddering breath and stopped crying altogether. Looking down, her tear-filled eyes were fixed on mine, looking somewhat confused at the situation. I slowly breathed out, afraid to set her off again. What had just happened? It wasn't the baby's fault, and I didn't think I had done anything to cause it. Either way, I knew that no matter what—or who—had caused this unexpected outburst, I was now completely and utterly on my own.

* * * * *

The next two weeks passed in a blur of sleep deprivation, diaper changes, and simply learning who my baby was and how to be a mom—her mom. Beth was kind, sympathetic, and patient with middle-of-the-night crying, but she couldn't help parent this child nor pitch in with feeding since I was breastfeeding. Late one night as Rachel slept, I took a hard look at the situation. There was no way I could take that job. I was too exhausted just being a mommy. I called the bakery the next day.

Like all newborns, Rachel required feeding and changing every two to three hours, around the clock. Bedding and nighties needed frequent changing, so the laundry piled up fast. I rarely cooked because I didn't care what I ate. Grocery shopping was impossible without the car seat I still needed to buy. It all added up to a crash course in responsibility, piled on top of hormones and a sadness I didn't understand.

Meanwhile, other strange problems cropped up like weeds. The first was bath time. I had taken parenting classes at the local community center and was pretty sure I knew how to bathe Rachel: fill the plastic tub with warm water; gather together the soap, washcloth, baby towel, and a fresh diaper before undressing her; cradle her neck and head in the tub with one hand so she would feel secure as I soaped and rinsed her hair and body with the other. Easy. Yet no matter how hard I tried to do everything just so or how carefully I timed her bath (not right after a meal or when she was sleepy), each and every bath produced a torrent of terrified tears.

Before each bath, she would happily lie on the blanket I would spread on the floor beside the tub. I would slowly unsnap the nightie and pull off each sleeve and pant leg, while she would eye me with growing suspicion. I would talk and coo at her as I undid the diaper pins, then slowly peel back the diaper's corners. Her suspicion by that time would always grow into full-fledged alarm. I would hold my breath and slowly lift her legs and bottom to pull the diaper out from under her, cringing as her breath came in short, panicky intakes of air. And then it would happen: I would lift her into the air; the diaper would slip off; and her sweet mouth would let out an ear-shattering wail of terror and outrage, which carried me back to our big hospital exit. Unnerved, I would wash her as fast as possible and wrap her tightly in a towel, and the tears would end.

At first, I thought it must be the undressing that she feared. But she showed no distress when I changed her diaper and clothes in the bedroom. Then one day it started to rain while we were outside. As each raindrop splashed her upturned face, she grew increasingly nervous and unhappy, then burst into an angry fit of tears. Clearly, she didn't like water—from the sky or in a tub.

Being alone was another trigger. She was fine in her crib or playpen if I was close by. But if left alone, she would immediately wail, refusing to amuse or comfort herself. Then an even more puzzling issue presented itself when I changed her one morning.

"What's that?" Beth asked as she came up behind me. Rachel had a dime-sized sore on her tummy.

"I don't know. It was just a tiny blister last night."

"That looks really bad," she said with concern.

I called the pediatrician Dr. Ewing had recommended and got an appointment that day.

"I've seen this before, but it's a rare condition," Dr. Elrich said. She was young and pretty and had a gentle demeanor I found comforting. She cleaned the sore, applied ointment, and covered it with gauze. "Your baby is allergic to the natural bacteria in her own sweat. It's something she'll outgrow as her immune system gets stronger, but this time of year the warm weather will cause more blisters. Keep her as clean and dry as possible, bathe her often, and apply this ointment whenever new blisters appear."

I didn't relish the prospect of extra baths, but what could I do? Her poor tummy was raw. I couldn't let it happen again.

For several days, I battled little blisters as fast as they appeared and became an expert at lightning-fast baths. Soon I felt like maybe I could handle this thing called motherhood—until the next crisis came along.

One morning I walked into the bedroom to see if Rachel was awake. When I got close enough to peek inside the crib, I saw that Rachel was on her back, eyes open. Our eyes met and she immediately broke into a toothless smile, warming my heart.

"Hello!" I said and scooped her up. I laid her on my bed to change her. When I took off the one-piece pajamas, I noticed a single long strand of hair wound tightly around the base of one toe, cutting off circulation.

"What is this?" I asked the squirming baby. "Where did that come from?"

I turned the pajamas inside out and immediately saw the culprit. They were secondhand pajamas that someone had given me. The fabric had static cling, and several hairs had somehow gotten caught and woven into the fabric that covered her feet. One of them had wound around her toe as she had wiggled in her sleep.

"Hold on, I'll have that off in no time." I got the round-ended baby scissors and tried to remove the hair without cutting her skin, but it was wound too tightly. I couldn't get the end of the scissors between the layers of hair and her toe. Meanwhile, the toe was starting to swell and turn purple.

"Baby girl, this isn't working. I need help."

Thirty minutes later we were in the emergency room of the same hospital where she had been born. The doctor on duty got right to work, but it didn't look like he was getting anywhere.

"If I don't get this off soon, I'll have to cut into the toe to work it free."

"Please don't cut her!"

"I'll try a little longer, but if I wait too long she may lose the toe."

Rachel was crying from pain and fear. Likewise, the doctor looked stressed; his brow furrowed in deep concentration. Tears sprung to my eyes as I silently prayed, willing the hair to come loose.

Several agonizing minutes later the doctor sighed with relief. "I've gotten under it," he said. He worked the tip of the scissors between the layers of hair and cut each one. He used tweezers to pluck and unwind the hair until it was completely off, then massaged the toe to restore circulation.

"Throw out every pair of old pajamas," he said. "This baby came very close to losing a toe. Saving a few dollars with used pajamas isn't worth that."

"Out they go," I promised.

Back at home, I examined all of her pajamas, socks, and booties. Anything that had hair caught in it was thrown away. That left a meager number of new pajamas, which meant doing laundry more often, but I didn't care. It never happened again.

For a short time after that, life settled down into a predictable routine. Rachel started sleeping longer, allowing me to get more sleep. I learned to nap when she napped, saving chores for when she was awake. Once again I thought everything was under control until our little train derailed again.

It all started with an unexplained soreness in my breast that made feedings painful. Within twenty-four hours, that initial soreness escalated to painful swelling, burning, and a spiked fever. I called Dr. Ewing and described the symptoms.

"Sounds like a milk duct infection. You'll have to stop breastfeeding while you take antibiotics. I'll warn you, your milk may dry up in that time. If it does, that's the end of breastfeeding."

Rachel switched to formula in a bottle—something she wasn't too happy about. With practice, she eventually got the hang of it. What I didn't expect was the sudden case of severe colic that came afterward. Starting with that first bottle, each feeding was followed a short time later with Rachel doubled over in pain, crying her heart out. When I tried to hold and comfort her, she would stiffen up like an unyielding board and push me away with doubled-up fists. I felt so helpless to do anything for her. And just as the doctor had warned, my milk stopped and never came back. So it was the bottle or nothing.

"What can I do?" I asked Dr. Elrich. "She's in so much pain every time she eats!"

"Colic is something that's difficult to trace to any particular cause," she explained sympathetically. "Most of the time babies just need time to outgrow it."

"But she never cried like this when I breastfed her. Why would she suddenly get colicky now?"

"I don't know. My advice is to try different brands and see if that helps. Also don't let her drink too fast. Other than that, patience and time are key. But let me know if it gets any worse."

"Patience and time"? Rachel is suffering! I was at the end of my rope. Was this platitude really my best option? Once again, Hal's words circled my weary mind like a taunting school-yard chant: *The enemy hates you; he knows the best way to get revenge is to go after your children. He seeks only to steal, kill, and destroy.* Not only did it feel like Rachel was under attack, my ability to mother her felt threatened as well. That night Satan filled the room with an unwelcome energy. While lying in bed, I could hear random sounds and felt his dark presence. With my guard down, the accuser hit his mark as I mentally analyzed my own inadequacies as a mom. I felt so defeated. The moon came into view through the window and then slid back into obscurity behind a cloud as I cried myself to sleep.

* * * * *

The next day I vowed not to give up. I tried every brand of formula in the house, then went to the store and tried others. Not one made a difference. Colic still twisted her little body with painful cramps. This went on for a couple of weeks until a miracle happened. Rachel got the flu.

"Give her Pedialyte [an electrolyte and rehydration solution]," Dr. Elrich instructed. "It's clear and will stay down better. When her fever is gone, give her soy formula before switching back to regular milk formula. Soy is easier to digest."

Her flu lasted for several days. As soon as the symptoms lessened, I gave her the soy formula. She seemed to enjoy it and drank every drop. As always, I burped her and lay her down in the crib, waiting for that first inevitable wail of pain from colic. But the cries never came. After several minutes, I brought her into the living room with me while I folded laundry. She was fine and had no signs of colic.

The next day I called Dr. Elrich to let her know. "Do you think it's the soy formula?"

"Maybe. Some babies can't tolerate milk formula. I suggest keeping her on soy from now on."

I couldn't help wondering why she hadn't suggested soy before. Knowing it wouldn't help to blame the doctor, I put the past behind us. Surely better days were ahead.

CHAPTER

7

As the fall air grew colder and winter approached, Rachel and I settled into a routine, while my social life took a back seat. Along with fatigue and stress, the demonic attacks that had been sporadic during my pregnancy were happening more often, chipping away at my faith and stealing my sleep. At the same time, I struggled to understand why Rachel was still so sensitive to everyday stimuli.

There were times, of course, when all was fine. One evening when several AA friends came over to visit Beth and I, Rachel lay contendly in my arms, then let out a series of adorably high-pitched sneezes. It caught me so off guard that I couldn't stop laughing at the delightful cuteness of her baby sneezes. I laughed so hard that I thought she might start to cry, but she just looked up at me quizzically until I settled down.

But more often than not, she seemed anxious and unsure. As a new and very young mom, I didn't know how to make her more comfortable and calm. When I tried, she often got fussier. Thinking the problem might be spiritual, I reached out to my pastor for help.

"Pastor Temple," I said, approaching him after the worship service. "Could we talk?"

"Sure," he said kindly. "I was just going to the library for a book. Why don't you come along and tell me what's on your mind?"

The one-room library was quiet and private.

"Pastor . . . um, you see . . . I have these demons that bother me at night sometimes."

Normally mild-mannered, the pastor looked startled. "Oh?"

"Yes. Well, that's what brought me to your church in the first place. I thought they were ghosts, but my friend Hal explained they were really demons. He showed me the Bible and said I had to find a church. That's how I wound up here. I was even baptized but at a different church."

He looked perplexed and concerned, but I pressed on, hoping he would understand. "Pastor, the attacks are getting bad again, and I think they might be bothering Rachel too. She gets so fretful and acts like she's afraid of so many things. What can I do?"

The pastor finally nodded as if he understood but was clearly uncomfortable with the situation. "Have you prayed, dear? Have you asked Jesus to intervene and to make them leave you alone?"

"Yes. I've prayed and prayed, but it keeps happening."

"I can see you're upset, but you know talking about demons just gives Satan license to harass you. I recommend you never bring this up again to anyone. Just keep praying in private until it stops. Will you do that for me?"

In that moment, hope shriveled up inside me and died. He wanted me to keep it a secret—just as I had kept my childhood abuse a secret—as though it wasn't happening.

"Sure," I said reluctantly. "If you think that's best."

"Good." Fairly beaming and looking relieved, he patted my arm. "You'll see, Cheryl. This is the best course of action, I'm sure of it."

* * * * *

One day after a meeting, I went to Pat's house to pick up Rachel. Tracy was helping.

"Cheryl, guess what? I've started Bible studies with the pastor so I can be baptized." Tracy handed Rachel to me. "I'm so excited to become a full member of the church."

I congratulated her then headed home, pondering her words. I had never considered what it took to become a member or if that was something I even wanted.

Back at home, I fed Rachel and put her down for the night. Beth was out with Paul, so I ate alone at the table and wondered where my life was going. I had learned the hard way not to date from the AA pool. There weren't any Christian men on the horizon anywhere. How old would Rachel be before one came along? I hated the thought of leaving her fatherless. It looked so dismal, especially with most of my family still so distant. The sheer loneliness of the situation was overwhelming. Would joining the church as a full member change anything? Would it bring my life into focus?

That night the victorious sneer of the enemy was palpable. I tried to believe that God's love would keep me safe and that He would provide a brighter future for Rachel and me. Sleep came, only to be interrupted again by the angry force of a demon holding me down. I struggled to fight off the usual panic until I could say the name of Jesus and beseeched God to make it all stop.

* * * * *

To take my mind off things and ease my loneliness, I started going to the church's Dorcas Society. Each week the ladies of the church made quilts and emergency kits. It quickly became a favorite outing for us, and I learned a lot from the other moms who brought their kids too.

Not long after that, another invitation pulled me further into the church's fold. "Would you like to come over for lunch?" Gayle asked after church. "We're having casserole and salad; there will be plenty for everyone. We want to get to know you better, and I'm dying to spend time with Rachel. She's so cute; I could just eat her up."

I was surprised at the invitation. I had always been shy, but I wanted to belong and feel as though I was a part of things. That meant saying Yes to things.

"Sure; that sounds nice."

"Great! Here's the address."

It was a fun afternoon. Gayle's family was affectionate and full of good-natured kidding—so different from my own family. Love permeated the home, along with dogs, cats, and birds. Everything about their home put me at ease.

After lunch, Jim and I discussed Seventh-day Adventist dogma and our limited understanding of it. Like Tracy, he was taking Bible studies.

"I want to understand the Bible better and why the church says No to some things," he said. "I was raised Mormon so I get not drinking coffee, but the rest is a mystery."

"Me too!" I said, happy I was not the only one with questions. "Do you want to get baptized?"

"I was baptized in the Mormon Church, but that's not the same. I'm considering it."

"I was baptized, too, with a friend. But it wasn't really my idea, so I'm not sure it counts."

"Maybe you should take Bible studies too. It may help you decide."

"I might, but I haven't made up my mind yet."

"Yeah, it took me a while to get there too. It will happen when you're ready."

His words were comforting, and I didn't even mind when Gayle asked about my family. They weren't trying to force anything. So when they invited me for more Sabbath lunches, I gladly accepted. Soon they felt like family. They even got Rachel a playpen for naps. It became our second home.

Before long, the holidays arrived. Just before Thanksgiving, Mom called with surprising news. "Your dad wants you and Rachel to come over this weekend so he can take pictures of her."

He hadn't seen the baby yet or even called. This invitation came out of left field. "Are you sure he wants us to come?"

"Of course. He's been fiddling with his camera all week, trying to figure out the best lighting and where you should sit."

"OK. Is Sunday all right? I have plans for Sabbath."

"Yes. Come around three. After he's done, we'll barbecue. Is chicken OK for you to eat?"

"Chicken is fine," I said, surprised she had thought to ask about my diet.

On Sunday morning, I tried not to think about Dad's previous rejections. Driving through the scorched canyon was a grim reminder of what we had narrowly escaped. When we crossed the little white bridge at the lake's entrance and passed the clubhouse, I was comforted by the lake's serene, unharmed beauty. The lake was still home.

"Hello!" Dad called with a wave. He had heard the car coming and rushed down the stone steps to meet us. "Here, let me help you with her." He took Rachel so I could carry her paraphernalia. "Aren't you gorgeous?" he cooed, smitten already.

For the next hour, my dad used an entire roll of film to forever document Rachel's infancy. His delight in her was obvious. Whether his heart had been softening for months or it had melted at the sight of her, I couldn't tell. But watching and listening to them interact and hearing his endless questions about her growth and progress made my own heart soften with forgiveness.

When he finished, we enjoyed the sundeck, eating and chatting until the sun slid behind the hills. I had missed feeling a part of my nuclear family, which made the day sweet. Later, after everything was cleaned up and put away, I started preparing to head home. Mom came from the kitchen with leftovers wrapped in foil and plastic containers to tuck in the diaper bag.

"You and Rachel are invited next Thursday for Thanksgiving dinner at Betty and Winn's house," she said. "Why don't you plan on getting to their house around five thirty? Dinner is at six."

Again I was stunned. Growing up, Aunt Betty and Uncle Winn had been my second parents. Betty taught me to read at her kitchen table. Winn's gentle, kindly manners had always made me feel special and safe.

"Why now?" I asked. "What changed?"

"I don't know," Mom said under her breath. "Just take it as an olive branch. Come for dinner, and see what happens. At least they're making an effort. Meet them halfway, OK?"

I thought back on how good reconciliation had felt that night.

"Fine, I'll meet you there."

* * * * *

Thanksgiving unfolded like a dog-eared letter from an old friend, read dozens of times. The long silent months were forgotten as the women worked in the kitchen making homemade holiday favorites, including Betty's canned applesauce for dessert, while the men talked sports in the living room.

When everything was ready, we reconvened in the living room and sat around the long table that was really just four card tables lined up and covered with a long cloth. Winn said grace in his quiet, humble way, and we dug in. Rachel sat in her infant chair, taking it all in with wide-eyed wonder.

Like Sunday with my parents, this night produced ample evidence that we were loved and wanted, albeit still misunderstood, by this family.

Over dessert, my uncle brought up the subject of work.

"I had a job waiting for me, but it was too hard to start a new job and care for a newborn at the same time. Now that she's older, I could sign up at a temp agency."

"Who'll watch her while you're working?" he asked kindly. Unlike my mother, Betty had always stayed home with their kids.

"A friend from church. She babysits Rachel when I attend meetings."

"Excellent." Winn gave me one of his kindest smiles, filling me with a warm peace and a sense that I was back in the fold and on the right track.

I relaxed after that as the conversation shifted to something else. His question had me thinking, though. It *was* time to start looking for work. The next day I called several agencies and made appointments.

* * * * *

The brisk December wind stung our cheeks as we went door-to-door singing Christmas carols for delighted homeowners. We gave out tracts, accepted donations, and asked neighbors if they wanted to receive Bible studies. It was the first good, clean fun I had experienced since childhood that didn't involve drugs, alcohol, or sex.

Finishing up at the last house of the night, we returned to church for buttered popcorn and hot chocolate. Upon entering the kitchen, I was surprised to see Pastor Temple, wearing a checkered apron and a big grin, pouring hot chocolate. He was alone, so I grabbed a plastic serving tray and headed his way.

"Hi, Pastor," I said while transferring the full cups on to the tray. "Could I ask you something?"

"Sure. What's on your mind?"

"I know you said not to talk about it, but I'm still having the same problem as before." He said nothing. "I was talking to Jim Mills, and he suggested I take Bible studies to clear some things up that I don't understand. Do you think that would clear up my other problem too?"

"It might," he said as he continued pouring. Clearly, this topic still made him uncomfortable. "Anything that helps you understand Scripture will build your faith and, in turn, help with any spiritual battles you may be facing. I'll talk to Daniel, the associate pastor. He'll arrange a time to meet for Bible study."

I liked that suggestion. It would be easier to talk things over with a pastor nearer my own age.

"Sounds like a plan," I agreed.

* * * * *

For the first meeting, Pastor Daniel and I met in Pastor Temple's office at the back of the church. It was a claustrophobic room, lined with books. Pastor Daniel sat behind a heavy desk. I sat in a small leather chair, watching shafts of light illuminate dust particles in the air. Rachel sucked her pacifier in my lap, fiddling with my long hair. It would be a miracle if she lasted the entire half hour.

"Cheryl?" he asked, sounding unsure.

My mind had wandered. "Sorry, Pastor, can you repeat the question?"

"Please, call me Daniel," he said kindly. "I asked how much of the Bible you've read."

I nodded, trying to refocus. For some reason, my mind felt befuddled as dark, unwelcome thoughts flitted through it. My attention span was unusually short that afternoon; it required tremendous effort to shut out erroneous thoughts in order to concentrate on his questions.

"Not much," I admitted. "Little bits here and there when Satan bothers me at night. And I try to look up verses during the sermons. I still don't really understand what I'm reading most of the time."

Daniel's eyebrow lifted. "Satan is bothering you?"

I sighed. Another pastor to convince. I shared the condensed version, including examples of past harassments at the lake and how demons attacked at night.

He nodded with a benign expression, apparently accepting my explanation.

"During the sermons, how do you look up verses?"

I opened the large leather Good News Bible Gayle and Jim had given me for Christmas and showed him the table of contents. "By the time I find which verse you're reading from, you've usually gone on to the next one. That's when I give up and just listen."

His brow furrowed, then he opened a drawer, pulled something out, and handed it to me. "Here, this will make your search easier."

I examined the sheet of colorful plastic tabs that were imprinted with the names of the books of the Bible. "How do they work?"

"They're sticky on one side. Just attach the appropriate tab to the first page of each book. That way you can find the book you want quickly."

"It's a cheat sheet!" I giggled.

"It's a time-saver. Eventually, you'll know the names of all sixty-six books and where to find them. In the meantime, this will eliminate frustration. As for verse numbers, they're simply a means of organizing the chapters of each book, paragraph by paragraph. Don't worry; you'll catch on soon enough. Now why don't we get started?"

He handed me the first lesson. It was small, just a few pages long. Each weekly lesson covered a different topic, such as faith, heaven, death, and so on. He explained that I would read and answer the questions at home, then go over them the following week with him. Rachel played quietly with her toys until we were nearly finished, then she let me know she was hungry and needed a change.

Watching her fuss, Daniel shifted gears. "I'm wondering where to meet next week," he said.

"What's wrong with here?"

"It's just a bit uncomfortable, especially for Rachel. Somewhere less formal might be better. What would you think about coming to our apartment? My wife, Faith, could fix lunch and help out with the lessons. Rachel could play with our daughter, Emily. They're both crawling now. The floors are carpeted. We have toys and books. What do you say?"

"Sure," I said, gathering up Rachel's stuff. "Same day and time?"
"I'll ask Faith. If she agrees, we'll eat at noon and do the lesson afterward. I'll let you know."

* * * * *

That next Sabbath Pastor Daniel said Faith was on board. After that, Tuesday afternoons were spent at their home. Faith made wonderful vegetarian meals, and at Daniel's proud prompting, she explained how she fed a family of three on a tight budget. To save more money, she sewed clothes for herself and Emily.

Faith added much to the weekly lessons by modeling hospitality and offering tips on motherhood. Since Emily was a few months older than Rachel, Faith filled me in on what was coming and what had worked for her. I learned how a young Christian family functioned and behaved with each other, giving me fresh hope for a family of my own someday.

We studied many topics, including lifestyle choices such as which days to work and the wearing of jewelry. This prompted discussions on job choices, dressing modestly, trusting God to provide work, and developing beauty that came from within. It had taken years to learn how to be attractive to the world. Now God was asking me to give up the usual tricks of outward allure. It was difficult, but gradually through Daniel's biblical knowledge and Faith's gentle wisdom, I gained a new perspective on what true beauty is. The Holy Spirit also worked to rid me of preconceived ideas about Christians. Over time, Daniel and Faith became friends as well as teachers. The only downside was that our time together would soon end.

CHAPTER

Our last lesson was on baptism. I explained that I had already been baptized. "I was baptized almost two years ago at another church—very spur of the moment. Is that enough?"

Daniel smiled. "In a way, yes," he said. "In other ways, no." He tossed a small toy to Emily, who squealed with delight, then continued. "Baptism is a public declaration that you're accepting the gift of salvation. It's a sacred promise that you intend to serve God from here on by following His precepts and will for your life. It is in fact a vow and not to be taken lightly."

I said nothing, trying to understand.

"A spur-of-the-moment vow with no understanding of what you were promising is like a flippant marriage to someone you don't know. In the end, you'll probably wind up divorced. Likewise, baptism without an informed decision probably won't lead to a lasting relationship with God. See what I mean?"

"So you're saying I'm married to God?"

"Kind of. The Bible refers to Jesus as the Bridegroom and the church as the Bride. When you are baptized, you enter into a marriage-like covenant that binds you to Jesus for eternity. It's a serious decision and shouldn't be made because someone is dragging you into it."

"Technically speaking, wouldn't I still be married to Jesus, even if I didn't exactly mean it at the time?"

Daniel laughed. "You could look at it that way. But if you decide to be baptized again in our church, it will be a deliberate, eyes-wide-open action on your part to *choose* God, rather than being shoved into a shot-gun wedding. It's also a tradition at our church to vote people in as new members right after baptism, so you need to decide if you want that as well."

I looked at them both and weighed my choices.

"As I said, it's a big step," he affirmed while rising. "Why don't you take some time to think about it?"

"OK." It was time to go. "I'll let you know soon."

* * * * *

That week Eric, a friend from AA, invited Rachel and me to dinner at his apartment with his dad, who was a TV news executive. The evening passed pleasantly, with Rachel captivating Eric's dad. Finally, he looked at me with a serious expression. "Cheryl, you've impressed me tonight. I'd like to offer you a job."

"Doing what?" I asked in surprise.

"I'm in charge of Eyewitness News for the West Coast. You name the job; I'll make it happen."

I knew nothing about the news. I rarely watched it on TV. I could write term papers, but that was it. I was camera shy, intimidated by large groups of people, and had little self-confidence. His proposition was terrifying; plus, any media job would require working on the Sabbath. If I did get baptized, that would be a problem.

"Thank you, sir. Your offer is very generous, and I'm honored. But Rachel is still so little. I don't think I'm ready to leave her with someone full time while I chase a career in broadcast news. I'm sorry."

He looked disappointed but managed a gracious smile. "Well, the offer stands, anytime. Eric knows where to reach me."

For days afterward, I thought about Eric's dad and Daniel's words about baptism. Never before had the decision to follow God seemed so monumental or life changing. As he had said, this was more than a choice—it was a promise to God. Even as a nonbeliever, I had always taken promises seriously.

Finally, I asked Pat.

"Baptism is a promise to try your best," she said. "It doesn't mean you won't ever make mistakes. I've made lots. We all do. Thankfully, God is always ready to forgive, so we can try again."

"So you think I should do it?"

"Cheryl, it only matters what you think. But yes, I do. It will settle things in your mind and make you feel like you belong at church. Besides, don't you want to go to heaven?"

She made it all sound so simple. "Yes; I just don't want to let God down by rushing things."

"You've taken Bible studies. How ready do you need to be? Tracy can't wait. I say go for it, then let God work out the rest. That's my advice, take it or leave it."

I laughed. She was right. It was time to swim or go home. "I don't want to live my life without God. That much I know. OK, I'll get baptized," I said. I was happy the decision was made.

That night I called Mom with the news.

"Are you sure?" she asked. "Going to church is one thing. Becoming a member is quite another."

"I've given it a lot of thought, Mom. I'm ready. Please be happy for me."

"I'm trying," she said resignedly.

"Will you come?"

"To the baptism?" Her voice sounded shrill.

"Yes. Hal is coming. Beth too. I want you and Dad to be there. Can you ask him?"

"I'll ask, but it's been decades since he's stepped foot in a church. Even our marriage was performed by a civil servant in Guam. Don't get your hopes up."

*   *   *   *   *

That Sabbath the church sanctuary was flooded with sunlight that streamed through the side windows and tall stained-glass panels behind the pulpit. I watched as Jim was baptized first. When Pastor Temple pulled him up, Jim glowed with happiness. I watched Gayle get misty eyed when the congregation said "Amen" and voted him in as a member.

Tracy went next, full of excitement. Then it was my turn.

This baptism was different. I knew exactly what I was doing and why. When I entered the tepid water, I felt welcomed by it, enveloped in a cocoon of new life. Like Jim, my joy was evident when I came back up. I spotted my mother in the back pew with Hal and Beth. Dad was absent, but that was expected. When the congregation voted me into the fold, their acceptance flooded me like warm sunlight. Pat was right. It felt really good to fully belong to God and be welcomed into my church family. It was a happy day for all. Satan felt deceptively far away.

Over the next few weeks, I floated in a honeymoon cloud, eager to get more involved at church. In fact, I felt so free that I figured the battle with Satan was over. It was time to focus on finding work. I had several interviews, but none led to a job. As a single mom with an infant, I was a risky hire.

One night after an especially harsh interview, I realized the honeymoon was waning. Yes, I belonged to God. I also still lived in a hostile world like everyone else. Life was just plain hard. Loneliness reared its ugly head and made me ache for a man to help me face the battles of life.

Satan watched my growing discouragement and took full advantage by filling my head with doubts. *You'll never support Rachel without welfare,* the voice in my head proclaimed. *You'll always be alone. You'll never find happiness.* When sleep finally came, it didn't take long for a demonic attack to follow. It was over quickly but brought tears. My baptism had not eliminated that problem. My rest was fitful for the remainder of the night as I pondered this truth, alone.

* * * * *

One day my bedroom phone rang as I was putting a sleepy Rachel down for a nap.

"Hey, what's up?" Carl asked. "Why are you whispering?"

"It's nap time. If she wakes up now, it will take forever to get her back to sleep."

"Oh," he said in the way people do who aren't parents. "Well, listen, this won't take long. I have time off at work soon and thought you could come for a visit. We could ski and go for drives in the country. It would be a nice break for you."

"Carl, I don't have money for a plane ticket. And what about Rachel?"

"Take the bus. I'll pay for it, and your ski rentals too. Just hop on a bus and show up. Rachel can stay with someone. It's only for a few days."

I sensed a hidden motive behind his generosity. Still, he was right. I was worn out in every way. The very thought of a vacation was heavenly.

"I'm not promising anything, but I'll ask Pat."

"Great! I'll call the bus line for departure times."

I hung up and went to the living room to think. A week was a long time to an infant. They grew and changed daily and had short, little memories. How would she react to a long separation? Would it throw her into a panic? Or worse, would she forget me? I needed to do something. I had grown numb from money worries and job seeking. My patience with Rachel had grown thin. Maybe a break would do us both good. I might even come home ready to tackle life afresh. I called Pat that evening. She said Yes.

It was an uneventful bus ride until we hit a blizzard in Salt Lake City, Utah. Our seasoned driver handled the bus with expert precision until it skidded sideways toward parked cars and shops. At the last possible second, he regained control. It was a bad scare. Was God trying to tell me something? Maybe this whole thing was a bad idea. It hadn't occurred to me to ask God if I should travel to Idaho.

Either way, it was too late to back out. Carl was waiting, and buses don't turn around. Once there I enjoyed Carl's quaint, small town. We visited his friends and attended meetings together like old times. Midweek we skied the Tetons and made snow angels. It was the fun break I needed. I missed Rachel, of course, and looked forward to going home to her soon. But I also felt refreshed, invigorated, and ready to face life head-on. That is, until Carl brought up marriage again.

"Why won't you marry me?" he asked with frustration. "I have a good job and tons of family up here. I could take care of you. You could stay home with Rachel and forget about needing a job. Besides, I love you. I would make a great father for Rachel. She needs a dad."

He was hitting all my buttons. I still wasn't in love with him, but I did love him dearly as a friend. I wanted someone in my life who would love both Rachel and me. Carl was right. She was growing up fast and needed a father. The longer I waited, the harder it would be for her to accept a new daddy. And I was so tired of carrying the entire load alone—a load that got heavier every day.

I looked into his kind, sincere eyes. Despite the knot of doubt in my gut, and without asking God what He thought, I swallowed hard. "OK. I'll marry you." And that was that. Life took another sharp turn. I only hoped it would lead to happiness and not regret. We set the date for an April wedding in Los Angeles. That gave us just weeks to get ready.

When I got back to Los Angeles and went to Pat's house, Rachel refused to leave Tracy's arms. She looked at me with angry, mistrustful eyes and burrowed deeper into Tracy's embrace, leaving Tracy embarrassed. I tried again, but Rachel's wails made the transference miserable for everyone.

"She's just tired," Tracy said. "She was about to go down for a nap."

"That's right," Pat rushed to agree. "She really missed you the first few days, but then she got used to being with us. It's an adjustment, that's all. She's probably confused."

It was a difficult homecoming. I was coming down with a cold, and Rachel didn't want my arms.

"I'm sorry, little one," I told her softly, trying to hug her close despite her stiff limbs. "I shouldn't have left you for so long."

Eventually, Rachel and I found our rhythm again. The key seemed to be routine, which I stuck to like glue. Again I wondered how much of this was spiritual in origin. Our mother-daughter relationship had been tenuous and fragile from the beginning, rarely easy or in tune with any kind of natural flow. Maybe having a daddy in the picture would help. She needed as much stability as I could create. Marriage seemed like the best way to achieve that and keep Satan at bay. I asked Beth to be my maid of honor, and we made plans to go dress shopping.

Then just four weeks before the wedding, the temp agency called with a two-week job at a commercial aircraft company. I needed the extra money for the wedding, so I took it. Dress shopping and wedding preparations would have to wait.

* * * * *

When the temp job was over, Babette had my mother, Rachel, and I join her and the women of her family for a bridal lunch at a posh Beverly Hills restaurant. We ate on the small terrace surrounded by lush flowers. Everyone was very cordial, and Babette did her best to bridge our cultural differences.

Afterward, Babette pulled me aside. "Next week I'd like you and Rachel to visit me at work."

I gulped. "Paramount Studios?"

She nodded, tickled at my surprise. "I'll take you around the entire lot, all the behind-the-scenes stuff that outsiders never see. Then we'll have lunch in the studio commissary. Doesn't that sound fun?"

"Sure; it sounds great. Thank you."

"Wonderful! It will give us a chance to make wedding plans too. I'm so excited to help! Let's make it Wednesday. I'll give you directions and leave your name at the front gate."

My head was spinning. She was trying so hard. Despite my discomfort, I was warmed by her efforts. If only we could stay in Los Angeles, so Babette and I could get better acquainted. But Carl was set on Idaho to be near his father. I would soon be leaving California and everything familiar to me.

* * * * *

On Wednesday morning, I pulled up to the main gate of the iconic Paramount Pictures Studios lot on Melrose Avenue in Hollywood. Even to a native-born Los Angeles girl, this was impressive.

"I'm here to see Babette Hall," I told the gray-haired security guard.

He raised his eyebrows, scanning the names on a clipboard. "And you are?"

"Cheryl," I said. Pointing to the car seat in back, I added, "And my daughter, Rachel."

His smile grew genuine as he took in the baby. He rang up Babette's office and announced our arrival. "Guest parking is over there. Welcome to Paramount! Enjoy your stay."

The gate magically swung open, beckoning us inside the hallowed ground. With a friendly wave, I drove in, parked, then got Rachel and her stroller out.

"Cheryl!" Babette's distinctive voice rang out across the parking area. She fairly sprinted to our car with a radiant smile. She looked beautiful and every inch the executive. My yellow spaghetti-strap sundress was casual in comparison. Rachel wore a white cotton dress with flowers in the pattern and a bonnet to shade her eyes.

"I'm so glad you made it!" She gave Rachel a quick kiss. "I've been telling everyone that I'm going to be a grandmother," she giggled. "I can't wait to show her off, and you both look adorable. This is going to be such a fun day."

We met her staff in the legal department and then saw the back lots where facades and trimmings created a variety of "towns" for every type of movie or TV shoot. We visited a screening room where a director was watching his film. Finally, it was time for lunch.

"The commissary is this way," she gestured.

I followed her lead. "This place is amazing. You must love working here."

"I do, but it's a lot of responsibility. It can get overwhelming sometimes." She walked several steps, then stopped and turned a piercing gaze my way. "You know, I've been thinking."

"About what?" I stooped to retrieve a pacifier Rachel had dropped on the walkway. I popped it in my mouth to clean it off and then put it back in hers.

Babette was amazed. "I wouldn't have done that for my boys. You're a good mom, Cheryl."

"Thanks," I smiled, taken aback by the unexpected praise. "So what were you thinking about?"

"Well, to be honest, I'm just not convinced this marriage is going to work out."

I took a sharp breath, nonplussed by her off-the-wall admission. "Why? I thought you were excited about it."

"Don't get me wrong, Cheryl. I'm not against it. I like you *very* much, and I adore Rachel. It's just that the more I get to know you, the harder it is to see you being happy with Carl, especially in Idaho!" She reached down to absently tickle Rachel's cheek. "You see, when I married Carl's dad, he insisted that we live in Idaho, too, and I just hated it! I missed my life in Los Angeles, and I think you will too. So when it doesn't work out—and it won't—I want you to come right back here to me." She made a sweeping gesture. "I'll give you any job you want at this studio. You have my word."

Shocked into silence, I stared at her. I couldn't figure out if she was insulting me or trying to give me a way out. Or maybe it was some kind of crazy test. In any case, I didn't appreciate it.

"It will work out," I said defensively. "You'll see. Carl is my best friend. I want to marry him," I said with conviction, ignoring the twinge of doubt quivering through my stomach.

"All right," she conceded and gave me a quick hug. "If you say so. But if not, well, my offer still stands. Now let's get something to eat!" She smiled broadly and led the way.

In the commissary line, we met the young cast members from *The Bad News Bears*, who cooed and made funny faces at Rachel. At the table, Babette pointed out movie stars eating nearby. Then she started talking about the wedding. She wanted to pay for the flowers and a short honeymoon. It was sweet but didn't fit with her earlier predictions of a doomed wedding and the promise of a job.

"That's very generous, Babette, but I need to check with Carl. I'll let you know soon."

Right on cue, Rachel started fussing. She was tired. I thanked Babette for the lovely day and then left the bewildering land of Oz the way we had come—through the gate and back to reality.

CHAPTER

9

"Why can't you marry us?" I asked Pastor Temple.

He sat behind his desk, searching for the right words. "It's against church policy to marry a believer to an unbeliever. If neither of you were members, I might have married you. But with your recent baptism, you're a believer in every sense of the word. By your own admission, Carl is not. Marrying you would violate Jesus' instructions that believers be equally yoked with other believers. *Both parties must share the same faith.*"

I followed his logic, but I had hated rules since childhood. My dad's temper and alcoholism had spawned illogical, unreasonable rules that changed with the wind. His brand of chaotic control made me rebellious and resentful of any authority that got in my way. I wanted the pastor to make an exception. Meanwhile, Babette's stinging prediction rang in my ears. What was everyone's problem?

"If someone else performs the ceremony, then can we get married in this church?"

"No," he said firmly, then softened at my distressed expression. "It's for your own good. Perhaps you should give this marriage more thought before going ahead."

I left sad and frustrated at the pushback I was getting. Besides Babette and the pastor, Pat, Gayle, and Jim had all expressed doubts, warning me to slow down and reconsider.

"I know you don't love him," Gayle said. "Are you afraid to be alone? Is that why you're marrying him? Or is it his rich family? That's no reason to get married!"

The naysayers were piling up. Late that night I wondered if they saw something I didn't. Soon enough that doubt switched to stubborn anger. *I'm not marrying Carl for his money,* I told myself. *He loves me. He's my best friend. I want companionship. I'll grow to love him. I know I will! Carl will be good to Rachel. We can find another way to get married.*

* * * * *

The days ticked down at a frantic pace as more barriers came up, starting with the flowers. Carl and I had accepted Babette's offer, so she made arrangements with a flower shop. All I had to do was go in and order them. I had lost two weeks to the temp job, so now it was down to the wire. There was only one day left to order them in time for the wedding, and that day was a Saturday. That meant breaking the Sabbath or foregoing wedding flowers. After church, I went looking for the shop but couldn't find it. With each circling of the block, I grew more certain that God was telling me, *"No, don't break the Sabbath. Go home. This wedding is a mistake."* In my typical fashion, I bore down and kept looking until I found it. Eventually, the Holy Spirit will step back and allow rebellion to break through His barriers. I ordered the flowers.

Later that night Mom helped me overcome another hurdle.

"I talked to the lake's club manager," she said. "As a club member, for fifty dollars you can use the clubhouse and lawn for the wedding, and the date you've chosen is available."

A week later Carl called with more news. "I found a pastor to marry us, and she's free that Sunday. She's Episcopalian."

Now we just needed the groom. He was riding his motorcycle to Los Angeles.

"I should get there Thursday night. The wedding is Sunday. That gives us all day Friday to get blood tests and a license. Piece of cake."

I laughed, knowing how insane his plan was. "If you say so. Hey, be careful. Slow down if there's bad weather."

"Don't worry! See you Friday, bright and early."

* * * * *

"Where did you say this place is?" I was trying to drive and look for addresses at the same time. It was Friday afternoon during rush hour in West Los Angeles. Carl had hit bad weather on the trip after all and gotten in very late. Now we had just two hours of daylight to get everything done. It was impossible.

"There," he said, pointing to a white building.

Once we were inside, the receptionist rolled her eyes at our request. "It takes twenty-four hours to get blood tests back. No rush orders."

Carl set his jaw and went to find a pay phone. He returned, smiling with renewed vigor and determination. "Stan can do the blood tests and process the paperwork today. No waiting."

"Is that legal?" I asked sharply.

"He said Yes. That's good enough for me. Let's go; his office is clear across town."

Once again I was in a race to beat the Sabbath. It was close to sunset when we reached Stan's office. True to his word, he got it done lightning fast. City Hall was next. Crossing the miles, I watched the sky go dark. Sabbath had begun.

Carl was oblivious to the Sabbath. We weren't on the same page, as the pastor had warned. Instead, Carl focused on Rachel, who was hungry. I watched his efforts to comfort her as I drove. He tried toys, her Binky, patting her arm—nothing worked. She wanted food.

"Never mind, I'll give her a bottle once we get the license, if we get the license. They close in five minutes." I started to pray for help, then stopped short. I couldn't ask God to do something against His will. Besides breaking the Sabbath, even I could see He was against this wedding. All those roadblocks proved it. In my typical self-will-run-riot mode, I pushed on and took care of it myself, without His help.

With mere moments to spare, we ran inside City Hall as they were getting ready to lock up.

The clerk smiled wryly. "Cutting it close, aren't you?"

Carl laughed. "Our wedding is Sunday."

Her eyebrows shot up. Without another word, she quickly processed our paperwork. "There you go," she said, handing over the hard-won license. "Have a happy life!"

* * * * *

Sunday dawned beautiful and mild, foretelling a perfect spring day at the lake.

I did my own hair and makeup, then studied my reflection. I looked nice. But something was amiss. Letting go of the internal facade at last, I admitted to myself that I didn't want to finish getting ready. I didn't want to marry Carl. This was a mistake. I could feel it.

Mom appeared in the doorway. "Almost ready?"

I nodded, instantly hiding my feelings. It was simply too late. My fate was sealed.

She tucked a wayward curl into place and smoothed my hair. "This is a big day for you," she said quietly.

"Sure is," I agreed, forcing a smile.

"I'll have Rachel fed and in her new red velvet dress in time for the wedding. Now get going. The girls are waiting for you in the Bridal Room to help with your dress."

* * * * *

The wedding went off without a hitch. About fifty guests attended the ceremony and brief reception. My friend Laura took pictures. There was no music or dancing. Then it was time to leave for our honeymoon. As always, Rachel stayed with Pat and Tracy.

Our quaint Spanish-style honeymoon cottage was nestled in the hills above Santa Barbara. It was covered in bougainvillea and boasted a wood-burning fireplace that we used both nights. Carl was loving and considerate, but it was disappointing for both of us that my feelings remained purely platonic.

Then it was time to head for Idaho. Carl hitched a U-Haul trailer to my Camaro, loaded it with his motorcycle, my belongings, and our wedding presents, and we were off. To make our family complete, Mom gave us a shepherd-mix puppy we named Boofa. We were on our way.

The first day of travel went smoothly, and we crossed California and the tip of Nevada. We stopped for food and bathroom breaks, especially for Boofa. Despite traveling with an infant and a puppy, we made good time until nightfall. In Utah, a storm slowed traffic. Soon the rain became sleet and then snow.

"Should we stop?" I asked Carl, who was driving.

"No, we'll be fine. It should let up soon."

Rachel was asleep, oblivious to the storm. We drove for miles. Instead of letting up, the storm only got worse, reminding me of the dangerous blizzard in Salt Lake City.

"Carl, this looks bad."

He sighed nervously, never looking away from the road. We were following a semitrailer dangerously close. If the truck stopped or slowed suddenly, we would rear-end it for sure.

"Why are you tailgating? Give him space!"

"I can't!" Carl sounded afraid. "I can't see the lines on the road. He can. This is the only way to make sure I don't drive off the road and land in a ditch."

I felt totally out of control. Was this payback for ignoring God's barriers to the wedding? Or was Satan using my rebellion to take our little family out in one fell swoop? Had he won after all? With nothing to lose, I silently begged God to protect us, to keep us safe through the blizzard, to lead us to safety, and to give our marriage, our family, a chance.

"As soon as I see an exit, I'll get off the highway and find a motel."

"OK," I squeaked out.

"We'll be fine," he said more gently, but his hands gripped the steering wheel for dear life.

At last, there was an exit with a motel right there, with its lights blazing in welcome. We were safe. I breathed a prayer of thanks. Soon we were all tucked in for the night, even Boofa.

"We should reach home tomorrow night," he assured me.

I couldn't picture it. Home was the lake, sunny beaches, and high-school buddies.

"Yes," I said with a wistful smile. "Home."

* * * * *

While I had been planning the wedding, Carl had found a rental house on the edge of town. It was small: just two tiny bedrooms that barely accommodated our bed and Rachel's crib, a living room, bathroom, and eat-in kitchen. But it was home.

I quickly found the only Seventh-day Adventist church in town. It was small and even farther out in the country than our house. I liked its homespun appearance, and the people seemed friendly. They welcomed us with smiles, even when Carl stayed in the car or smoked before coming inside. Like most new relationships, these happy first impressions didn't tell the whole story. That unfolded later.

On my third or fourth Sabbath visit, I went to the Mothers' Room because Rachel was teething and fussy. Another mom was there with an equally fussy boy about Rachel's age.

"Hi," she said with a smile. "I've seen you around, but we haven't met. I'm Samantha, and this is Pete. My husband is Leo, one of the elders. My parents are Fred and Ruth. Did you move here recently?"

I introduced myself and explained that we had moved from Los Angeles where I had recently been baptized. Like Babette, she conveyed a polished self-assurance that was daunting.

"Don't worry. I won't bite," she said, winking. "But I have to ask, which side are you on?"

"Side?"

"Are you on the jewelry side or the no-jewelry side?" She glanced down at my left hand. Carl had given me a watch in lieu of a wedding ring. "I'm guessing the no-jewelry side."

"I don't know what you're talking about."

"Really? I thought everyone knew—even new people like yourself."

She went on to explain that half the church was against wearing jewelry of any kind, except a watch for telling time or a brooch for securing a dress or blouse. They felt it was a sin to wear any other form of jewelry, even wedding rings. The other half believed that wearing jewelry was a choice and not a sin. The pastor and his wife tried to stay above the fray and let each member follow their own conscience. Like Switzerland, they stayed neutral. Because of that, the members against wearing jewelry wanted him to resign so they could get a new pastor who would agree with them.

Her explanation was confounding. I had always worn jewelry, including toe rings. I had even triple-pierced my ears. It had been hard to give up jewelry when I joined the church; the last to go were the toe rings. I had tossed them at Mom's dining table on the way to the hospital and missed. They had fallen through a heating grate in the floor, never to be seen again. Harder still had been asking Carl for a wedding watch. He could have had his pick of family jewels to pass on to his new bride—something I had dreamed of as a young girl. I had always wanted a diamond engagement ring; instead, I got an inexpensive watch.

Difficult or not, no one made me give up jewelry in order to join the church. I chose to give it up, albeit for legalistic reasons. I thought I needed to in order to earn salvation by pleasing a stern God. Now Samantha was telling me that half her church—my new church—was waging war against the other half by trying to oust the pastor and force their views on the entire congregation. A church split was unfathomable, like an impending divorce in God's family.

"Can they do that?" I asked.

"They're sure trying! So far, the conference hasn't disciplined the pastor for his views. To force the issue, the no-jewelry side is making life miserable for the pastor and his wife so he'll quit."

"That's so mean! Christians are supposed to be loving and kind. How can this happen in a church?"

"Oh, you don't know the half of it. They have potlucks in their homes without inviting the pastor. They say unkind things behind his back; it's a nasty business." She shrugged in mock defeat. "So back to my original question. Which side are you on?" She smiled, but her eyes were all business.

My heart broke for the pastor and his wife. They were near retirement age and seemed like kind, gentle folk.

"Neither. I won't take sides! I like everyone I've met here so far, and I'm not interested in a fight. But off the record, I think each person should decide for themselves. No one can tell someone else what they can or can't wear. This is a church, not a dictatorship."

Sam gave me a quick squeeze of affection. "Well said, Cheryl. I'm with you! I like people from both camps. I just don't like what they're doing. From this point on, you and I are on the same team, no matter what label people give us!"

* * * * *

Once we were settled in, I did my best to call Idaho home. I planted corn in our large backyard; took long walks with Rachel; explored the countryside with Carl, including underground caves where we encountered bats; enjoyed retro movies at a historic movie theater that played organ music; and played board games. I taught Carl to cook more than coffee and peanut-butter sandwiches. He taught me how to write checks. It was a simple life, sans romance and passion. Together, we dovetailed our patterns of daily life.

I also got better at pinching pennies. Carl's family may have been wealthy, but we were not. We relied heavily on corn from our garden and vegetables our friends shared from theirs or gleaned from big farmers in town. Carl's father did well as a doctor, but the town had little commerce beyond the hospital and local retail shops, especially after the sugar-beet factory closed. Carl's job at Sears paid the minimum wage. Many times I shopped for groceries with just ten or twenty dollars in my purse—far less than I had spent down south when I had food stamps. But I wanted to stay home with Rachel. I remembered Faith's example and found ways to scrimp, such as baking bread at home and freezing veggies for later.

Another way I saved money was by switching to a vegetarian menu, which was something Carl didn't appreciate. I had scant knowledge of vegetarian cooking, so our diet was rarely nutritionally complete. To help, Mom sent recipes from the newspaper and a giant wheel of cheddar cheese that we used for weeks. Living on scarce resources was a challenge, and I worried about Rachel getting enough of the right kinds of food. To keep up everyone's morale, I touted the health benefits of being vegetarian. Inwardly, I longed for the bountiful table I had grown up enjoying.

As a married woman, I no longer slept alone. Even so, demons still invaded my nights. My solution was to cling even harder to legalism in the hopes that a strict, Adventist lifestyle would banish them and ensure my salvation, which often felt tenuous at best. The stress added up. When it got bad, I would crave cigarettes, especially when Carl smoked.

Sometimes after fighting off a demon, I would lie awake beside Carl, who always slept peacefully. In the dark, the enemy would remind me of past sins or the sketchy reasoning behind our marriage. I would worry that I wasn't good or pure enough for God and His kingdom in heaven. Every unkind word I had uttered that day, each tiny temptation given into would replay in my mind, breeding guilt that left me spiritually adrift. So I would resolve to try harder, find more worldly things to give up and more ways to atone for sins and earn God's favor. Temptation and sacrifice, hot and cold, back and forth: I struggled to obey God's laws to the letter. The trouble with living like that is that I never got there. I could never be perfect enough, so I always felt like a failure.

Carl suffered, too, under our harsh lifestyle, all in the hope of pleasing me. The final straw came when I suggested he cut back on tobacco to save money and for health reasons.

"I don't drink alcohol; you won't let me eat meat; and now that you've given my TV away, I can't even relax with a show," he complained one night. "Don't tell me I have to stop smoking too. Just because *you* have to be perfect doesn't mean I have to!"

His words stung. I had pushed him too far. To counter his frustration, I asked if we could get to know God better by reading the Bible together at bedtime. He agreed and gradually started attending church more. Then Fred and Ruth opened the door of hospitality by inviting us to an informal Bible study at their house. They served snacks, and other men attended. To our surprise, we both enjoyed it.

After that, Carl complained less, but we still struggled. Between my legalism and Satan's persecution, Carl felt more condemned than saved. He also suffered the ongoing hurt of my strictly platonic love for him, wanting my whole heart. I saw it in his eyes and heard it in his voice, which deepened my sense of guilt and failure.

Finally, I asked Ruth for advice. "How can I learn to love my husband more?"

We were alone, setting tables for a church potluck. Ruth set down the plates.

"I'll tell you a secret. I didn't love Fred when I married him."

"Then why did you marry him?"

"I knew he was a good, kind man and would be a good provider. You know there aren't many Adventists in these parts. We're the only Seventh-day Adventist church in a forty-mile radius. My prospects were slim, and I wasn't getting any younger. I knew he loved me. So I said Yes."

"Sounds like Carl and me, except he isn't Adventist."

"It wasn't an easy start. We rarely fought, but I didn't feel much for him either. That hurt him."

"You've been married a long time. Something must have changed."

Ruth smiled wistfully. "I changed. I asked God to change my heart and fill it with love for Fred. I made up my mind to hang in there until He did."

"Do you love him now?"

"Oh yes, dearly! But it took time. Have patience, Cheryl; trust God to help you with this."

"But Ruth, God didn't want me to marry him in the first place! Why would He help now?"

"Because He's a loving, merciful God. He is in the business of forgiveness and second chances. He wants you to be happy! Plus, He hates divorce. My advice? Lean on Him, and don't give up. You'll see."

Her words lingered for weeks. Our one saving grace was that Carl and I were still best friends, and married life was at times a fun adventure. As I had hoped, it felt good to have someone to share a home with, plan and joke around with, and share the joys and responsibilities of raising Rachel. So despite the lack of romance, I tried giving our marriage a fair shot.

* * * * *

I was doing dishes one afternoon when the kitchen got noticeably darker. A storm was brewing. Wind gusts whipped the corn stalks, and lightning bolts split the leaden sky, then came booming thunder. Carl was doing a crossword puzzle in the living room while Rachel napped. I slipped outside. I had always had a passion for storms and couldn't resist my first Idaho thunderstorm.

Perched on the back steps, I let the cloudburst drench me in delicious torrents of rain, as I reveled in the experience. I could feel how big and powerful God is and how small and helpless I was. In the midst of the storm, I felt caught between God and Satan, good and evil, like a fragile rope in a tug-of-war. It reminded me of a time when I was living in the guesthouse as a teenager and experienced a similar feeling of being caught in the middle of something bigger.

It happened on a Saturday night. I was drawing and had felt anxious all night. When I needed a pencil in the closet, something kept me from going in—something sinister that made me afraid. The guesthouse crackled with a bad energy. The "ghost" didn't show itself, but I knew I wasn't alone.

Days later a friend explained what had happened in the guesthouse that night. She had watched me by practicing astral projection (mind travel). I didn't believe her until she accurately described in detail what I had done, which songs I had listened to, even the horse picture I had drawn.

"High above you, two angels fought with swords. One was mean looking. His side of the room by the closet was darker than the rest of the house. The other angel was all in white. His side of the room was brighter. He looked like a good guy, but they were both angry at each other. They were fighting over *you!*"

I hadn't understood her vision of angels then. But after studying with Daniel, I realized that an angel of God and a demon had been fighting over me long before I knew Jesus existed. In fact, God saved me countless times in my "before Christ" years: I was shot at, nearly raped, almost drowned, walked within inches of a cliff I didn't know was there in the dark, overdosed on drugs—and yet I still lived to find Him.

Now, in the midst of a raging thunderstorm, I understood that Jesus and Satan were still fighting over me, and I wasn't at all sure who would win. Unnerved, I ran back inside, dripping wet.

"You're crazy," Carl lovingly teased while handing me a towel. I reached to take it, but he playfully snatched it back, then took over the job of gently drying my arms, face, and hair. I quickly changed clothes, then joined him on the couch to help him finish his crossword puzzle.

After the storm passed, I went to the store, leaving Rachel with Carl. When I got home, he met me at the door. "Cheryl, our baby had a seizure!"

"What? She's never had one before!"

I brushed past him. When I opened her room's door, Rachel pulled herself up by the railing and fussed to get out of her crib. I picked her up for a quick inspection. She looked fine.

Carl followed, looking worried. "Hon, I swear she had some kind of fit!"

"Like what exactly?"

"She was shaking, arms and legs out straight and stiff. She cried in spasms."

I examined her more closely. Her eyes were damp. That was all.

"Maybe she had a nightmare. She's OK now."

He scowled. "I'm telling you, something was *wrong*! I think we should take her to the hospital."

I talked him out of it, though he remained convinced the problem was medical. I believed that if something did happen, it was spiritual in origin. There were no more seizures after that, making me more certain than ever that the tug-of-war I had felt in the thunderstorm now included Rachel. Carl was right. Something was wrong, and something should be done about it. But what?

CHAPTER

10

"Carl, I need money for rice cereal and baby food." It was fall. Our corn and the produce we had gleaned throughout the summer was gone except for a dwindling remnant in the freezer.

"I don't have cash, but I get paid today. I'll go by the store after work."

I looked at him with narrowed eyes. "What happened to the twenty dollars you had two days ago?"

His expression turned guilty. "I bought lunch at the diner."

"Why? I made you two peanut-butter-and-honey sandwiches, like always."

"I just wasn't in the mood. I wanted meat, OK?"

"Twenty bucks on *meat?*"

"If you must know, I had bacon and eggs, pancakes, and *real coffee*. Not Postum! The rest went for cigarettes and the donation basket at last night's AA meeting. Satisfied?"

No, I was stunned. "So while Rachel gets by on the little bit of cereal we have left and I'm eating peanut butter for lunch, you're out buying bacon and cigarettes. Are you the only one that matters?"

His shoulders drooped. "Of course not. I just get sick of working so hard with nothing to show for it but a brown-bag lunch! It gets old. I'm sick of vegetarian food."

In a way, I understood his point. It was hard to give up so much all at once. Our diet was so mundane and repetitive that eating had lost its pleasure.

"I get it, Carl. But you can't be so selfish behind my back. It's not fair."

He offered a hug and raised his sack lunch in solidarity. "I'll work on it."

I sighed as he drove away. Marriage was hard work. Each argument felt like a step backward, causing wounds and self-recriminations. Some days, it was all I could do to hold on by sheer willpower. But Carl meant well. I sometimes wondered if our marriage had more romance and passion, then maybe I wouldn't need to work so hard at overlooking his faults. After all, I wasn't perfect either. He allowed me room for mistakes and shortcomings. I knew I couldn't manufacture romance out of thin air, but even so, I silently vowed to stop being so judgmental and be a more loving wife; that is, until he did something that pushed me over the edge.

* * * * *

"I went to the bank today." We had just finished an early dinner of beans and rice. It was time to ask Carl the question I had held in all evening.

"So?" he asked, looking uncomfortable.

"They said we have forty dollars in our checking account. You told me yesterday we were down to less than ten dollars until payday."

"What's the difference? I told you that so you wouldn't spend it. We need a cushion."

"We need food! Not to mention we're practically out of toilet paper. How could you lie to me like that? Don't you trust me to be careful with money?"

He slammed down the newspaper and jumped to his feet. "You're making me crazy! I work my butt off at a lousy job and try to do what's right. All *you* do is give me a hard time! Our whole life is nothing but church and religion and the Bible—don't eat this, don't watch that, stop smoking so much. What else are you going to take away from me?"

It was the same old argument, and I was sick of it.

"Nothing! I'm tired of trying to make a Christian out of you."

He was pacing, getting ready to bolt. I beat him to it.

"I'm going for a drive," I said, grabbing the keys and a sweater.

"Fine," he said through gritted teeth, with his eyes hard and his arms crossed. "While you're at it, why don't you ask God for a miracle, cuz we're gonna need one!"

I revved the Camaro and took off with an angry roar, aiming east toward the mountains. The miles flew by as tears coursed down my cheeks to the beat of Electric Light Orchestra on the eight track. I was oblivious to the fall colors; puffy, white clouds; and the deep-blue sky. Life was too hard to bear with nothing but willpower. My heart was growing harder by the day; and my walk with God a trial, with little joy to soften the blows. Old boyfriends looked pretty good in the rearview mirror, as did other severed relationships I had left behind for God. Just as the children of Israel longed for Egypt while they were in the wilderness, I ached for the simpler days of old, conveniently forgetting the emptiness of those days and the scariness of living with emboldened demons. I only remembered the freedom of fun times at the lake with friends: swimming, boating, hiking, jumping off the rope swing into the refreshing water. I wanted to drive away from my life, back to the way it used to be.

By sundown, I was tired. I turned off the road to stretch and calm down, parking in an area where our church group had picked mulberries that summer. Now bikers claimed the spot. Men and women stood around a campfire, drinking beer and talking.

They stopped to beckon me over.

"Hey there, little lady," one man said. "Want a beer?"

They looked so much like the friends I had been reminiscing about in the car; older, perhaps, and rougher around the edges, but similar all the same. An irresistible urge pulled me to join them, even as a still, small Voice warned against it.

"No, but I'll take a cigarette."

The man eagerly pulled one from his pack and proffered it, flicking his lighter. I leaned in to light it and pulled smoke into my lungs, fueling the rebelliousness within.

"Thanks," I said, smiling at the group.

For several minutes, I shed the fetters of faith and family. At first, it felt delicious, like scratching a persistent itch. But after a while, the fun faded, and a sting lingered behind the itch. The evil beneath became plain. Their coarse jokes offended, as did their leering. Sin lost its appeal. It was time to go.

Back down the mountain I went, totally spent. I no longer wanted what the bikers had to offer. At that moment, I didn't want home or Carl either. Out of options, I spent the night in a cheap motel, paying by check.

The next day I arose with new resolve. I had to grow up, face the life I had chosen, and make the best of it. Rachel didn't need to hear fighting or feel tension filling the house. So I went home full of repentance and apologized for staying out all night. I would try harder; do better; leave the past behind; make love grow where it didn't exist—be perfect.

* * * * *

A few days later I got out of the shower, eager for bed. I planned to start a novel I had picked up at the thrift store. Rachel was asleep. Carl had gone to a meeting with his friend Roger and wouldn't be home for another thirty minutes. I wrapped a towel around myself and headed toward the bedroom.

Suddenly, I heard an odd noise outside. Muted voices argued in the driveway on the far side of the house. I stopped to listen and wondered why Boofa and Carl's dog Rebo weren't barking.

As I stood there dripping, the voices got louder. They were coming closer. Soon they were right outside the front door, mere feet away. Terrified, I grabbed the phone from the wall and dialed Roger's house. His wife, Sandy, answered.

"Is Carl there?" I said in a stage whisper.

"Yes. What's wrong?"

"Get Carl!"

Seconds later, he came on the line.

"What's going on?"

"Come home, *now!*" I whispered louder.

Just then, someone on the other side of the door grabbed the doorknob and twisted it back and forth, rattling the flimsy door harder and harder. There was no deadbolt. It could fly open at any second, exposing me to predators. The demons of hell were pounding their way in. Satan was out for blood.

"Someone's breaking in!" I said louder. "They're at the front door!"

"Cheryl," he said calmly and deliberately. "I'm ten minutes away. Put down the phone, and get the rifle from our closet. It's loaded. Just aim it at the door. If they break in, they'll be greeted with a loaded rifle. That should keep you safe until I get there."

"I don't know how to shoot it!" I cried, watching the door shake on its hinges.

"You won't have to shoot. They'll get the message."

I secured the towel and got the rifle, aiming it straight at the door. Outside angry curses rang out as they gave it their all. Miraculously, the old door refused to give way as I prayed with all I had, hoping God loved me enough to save me and the baby sleeping soundly in the next room.

After a minute, they gave up. The door stopped moving. Footsteps retreated into the night. Even so, I never moved, just in case they came back. Several agonizing minutes later a key turned the lock, and the door opened. It was Carl.

He looked amazed. I was still wet and shivering, with the rifle held defiantly high.

"You can put that down now, hon," he said gently.

I lowered it, allowing him to lean it against the wall. I fell into his arms and sobbed in relief. He was home. I was so glad to see him and to let him hold me. We were all safe. He held me a long while, letting me calm down before we fell on to the couch.

"You did great, hon. I'm proud of you. But tomorrow we're going to the mountains for target practice. You need to be able to protect yourself and Rachel."

"Did you see them? Were they out there?"

"No, they're gone. But they broke into that old truck the landlord left behind. They went through the glove compartment and pulled everything out."

"Why didn't the dogs bark?"

"They must have let them out while you were in the shower. I'll have to go find them before going to bed."

God had protected us. Still Satan felt menacingly close. So I agreed to learn how to shoot, even though I hated guns and violence. Through it all, I wondered when his persecuting revenge would end. When would I find a measure of joy and feel safe from Satan's long, angry reach?

* * * * *

"We have a problem," Carl announced one evening. A late September wind blew outside. He looked worn out and rubbed tired eyes as he flopped in a chair. "Our landlord skipped town and left no instructions on how to pay the rent. I don't think he wants to be found."

"We could just stop paying until he comes back."

"No. I think we should move as soon as possible, on our own terms. There are three lots for sale on the next block. A developer is going to build low-income housing. I think we should look into it."

"Carl, how can we buy a house when we're struggling to pay the rent?"

"Let's just see. Maybe there's a way. I'm sure my mom will lend us part of the down payment. If your parents help, too, we might be OK if the payments are low enough."

Despite our marriage feeling as fragile as glass, we ignored wisdom, and with help, bought the new house through a low-interest subsidized loan. The payments were close to what we had paid in rent, plus extras such as water and trash disposal. Amid moving boxes and general chaos, we celebrated Rachel's first birthday with cake and balloons, then gathered up our humble belongings and moved one block over to our brand-new split-level house.

The extra expenses meant I needed a part-time job. I got work in a nursing home and found an elderly couple to watch Rachel when Carl couldn't be home with her. Gradually, we fixed up the house with some help from Carl's job: discounted wallpaper for the kitchen; a new refrigerator for ten dollars, which had been dinged during unpacking; and a wood-burning stove that was marked down when someone scratched the back. I also got Chester, a cheerful yellow canary that sang in the kitchen all day.

The house was slowly coming together. For weeks, I plugged along, getting used to my new surroundings and responsibilities. Fall gave way to winter, adding the new challenges of frigid temps and icy roads. I didn't like driving in snow. That and the mundane, repetitive nature of my job made it tough to face work some days. But I would have kept going simply for the paycheck, if not for one cantankerous resident.

The day started out fine. After serving breakfast, I went to collect trays from the rooms. Coming out of one, I inadvertently startled an old man walking down the hall. He cried out, stepped back, and punched me hard in the chest.

Winded, I landed hard and stared up in surprise.

He glared back with rage. His eyes reminded me of the demon that had once sat on me in bed during an attack. Before I could speak, the old man shook his fist and yelled, "That ought to teach you!"

Fighting tears, I got up and brushed past him, straight to the boss's office to quit.

Finding that job had taken a long time. In the middle of winter, I would never find another one fast enough. With our heating bills going up, I needed to replace that lost income right away.

Trying to help, Ruth offered to let me shadow her while she worked as a colporteur selling Adventist books door-to-door. We enjoyed our day together, and she even made a sale. But it wasn't for me, especially because it required even more driving in winter conditions than my old job. After some discussion, Carl and I settled on me running a day care. I knew Rachel's elderly babysitters made more per hour than I had in the nursing home. An ad in the paper soon resulted in two babies coming regularly, which was enough.

During the winter months, Fred and Ruth took a hiatus from their weekly Bible study, but another couple, who lived way out in the country, soon took up the mantle. I convinced Carl to go, but the arctic wind made my nose hairs freeze between the car and their house. Once inside we enjoyed the study and fellowship and were tickled when the couple sent us home with two kittens, adding to our menagerie. But it was just too far to go in the dead of winter. We didn't go again.

That first Christmas in the new house, we enjoyed opening up a handful of gifts and eating a luscious fruit cake a neighbor had baked. Then Carl got out his tennis shoes, put them on Rachel's tiny feet, and led her awkwardly around the house. She'd already learned to walk, but this fun challenge made us all giggle.

Tuckered out at last, she flopped down in defeat. That's when Carl brought out her surprise: brand-new, black patent leather shoes—a present from Babette. Like the proud papa he had become, he carefully slipped them on her feet and buckled them securely.

"I got new shoes!" she squealed with delight.

It was a fun day, a bright interlude that brought a small measure of hope to us all, at least for awhile.

* * * * *

Meanwhile, even though we still fought with stubborn frequency, Carl was showing more interest in reading the Bible. One night as we read Matthew 24, he suddenly sat up.

"This is serious!" he said. "We have to tell people Jesus is coming!"

He sounded so sincere, it brought tears to my eyes.

"That's what I've been trying to tell you. I want all three of us to be ready."

After that, Carl decided to tithe his next paycheck. "It's only ten percent. Let's see what happens!" Perhaps this change was motivated by the twenty-dollar bill we had recently found in the park after I tithed my own weekly pay. In any case, he was putting God to the test.

Just days after paying his first tithe, Carl came running upstairs from the basement, waving something. "Look! A ring I lost years ago! I was cleaning out my old desk, and this was stuck behind a drawer. I never liked it anyway. We can sell it for more than I paid in tithe. It worked, Cheryl; tithing worked!"

I hugged him. "That's wonderful, Carl. I told you God is real. Now you see for yourself that He loves us and rewards obedience."

I was happy for him. Yet even as I watched him go back downstairs, I couldn't help wondering if Satan would find a way to keep Carl from trusting God completely.

It didn't take long to find out.

* * * * *

Samantha and her husband invited all the church members for a New Year's Eve party. It was a smashing success, even though none of the no-jewelry people attended. Every floor of their elegant home was filled with people playing board games, eating, and singing along to Christmas music. It was our first real Christian party, and I was impressed that so many people of every age and economic background could have so much fun together without alcohol or drugs. I also noticed the pastor's wife looked tired. She smiled and was friendly, but something was wrong. They left early while the rest of us rang in 1980 with noise and good cheer.

Not long after, I heard the news. Stress, strain, and heartache from all the infighting and rejection had taken a toll. The pastor's wife had suffered a heart attack and nearly died. That was enough. The pastor resigned. When she was strong enough, they left town for good.

"How could the church let that happen?" Carl demanded one night. "They were good people! She almost died, and for what? Because some knuckleheads have a thing against jewelry? That's nuts! You're always saying how good God is and how Christians are nicer than other people. Well, I know a lot of people in AA and at work who are a lot nicer than that bunch of holier-than-thou hypocrites. How is it wrong to wear jewelry, but OK to be cruel to people who don't agree with you? Why should I keep tithing at a church that acts like that or stop eating food that I like just because they say I should? You do what you want. I'm going back to being me."

"They're not all bad. Everyone at the New Year's Eve party was really nice. You said so yourself."

"Yeah, but they still keep going to church with those nutjobs. What's up with that?"

When I couldn't answer, Carl took his frustration out on the snow that needed shoveling. Inwardly, I felt the same way. The people who had broken the hearts of the pastor and his wife were no better—worse even—than the worldly people I had walked away from to join the church. If this was Christianity, I wasn't sure I wanted it anymore. What those people had done was unconscionable. I knew it wasn't God's fault. But if His rules were this harsh and unyielding, I wasn't sure I could follow Him with my whole heart. But what was the alternative? Satan? The mere thought gave me shivers. Was there a middle ground somewhere—a spiritual Switzerland? I didn't know anymore.

* * * * *

January brought more snow than I had seen in my life. I gradually adapted to below-freezing temps and brutal wind-chill factors, but there were days I wanted to stay under my electric blanket till spring. I was a beach bunny, not a snow bunny. I had already gotten stuck once at the market near our house, making Carl dig out the car. After that, he used my car for work instead of his motorcycle, which made my world even smaller.

Consequently, the only social outing left was church. We hadn't gone since the New Year's Eve party, and I was getting hungry for spiritual food and fellowship. Finally, I asked Carl to take us.

"I'm not in the mood," he snapped while staring at his cereal.

"Carl, it's snowing. I'm afraid to drive in snow. Please take us. They're having potluck this week."

He shook his head; his eyes were like chipped ice.

"Forget it. Maybe when they get a new pastor and figure out how to act like normal people but not now." He took his bowl to the sink.

A nasty argument followed, with shouting and hurtful words that couldn't be taken back. He angrily accused me of wanting to leave him for sunny Los Angeles. I was sure I could never look to him as the spiritual head of our family. We were at an impasse, and we both knew it. Shedding angry tears, I stomped to Rachel's room to dress her.

At her door, I turned to face Carl at the other end of the hall. "Never mind! I'll drive us since you won't. We don't need you!"

"Fine! Here's the keys!" He hurled them at me as hard as he could.

In a knee-jerk reaction, I slammed the door just in time for the keys to hit the door instead of me, making Rachel wail in terror. When I opened it, the door had a large hole in it. I turned and sat on the bed to hold Rachel as we cried together, with church forgotten. Carl snatched up the keys and slammed out of the house to drive away into the storm.

Two hours later he returned, bearing donuts. He apologized for throwing the keys. I made hot tea, and we shared the treat but said little to each other for the rest of the day.

When I started cooking an early dinner, Carl came up to me, looking lost. He wrapped his arms around me for a hug and buried his face in my hair.

"I do love you, Cheryl," he said earnestly.

"I know you do," I responded, unable to tell him I loved him in return. Despite my earlier resolve to patiently let God grow love where there was none, I was ready to give up. Understanding my unspoken message, he slowly let his arms fall disconsolately at his side and walked away. An hour later he left for the evening shift.

* * * * *

That night I pulled out a needlepoint project I had started in Los Angeles; it was a large reproduction of *The Reader* by Jean-Honoré Fragonard. While I made careful stitches on the canvas, I listened to an old-time radio mystery complete with creaky doors and sudden screams from victims in distress.

Rachel was asleep in her room. The snow fell steadily outside, blanketing the house with quiet. I relished the peace until I suddenly noticed that the light in the living room had dimmed slightly. The house, so quiet before, started emitting odd noises here and there. The peace vanished and was replaced by an evil presence. Sounds from Rachel's room grew more distinct and then louder. Something was wrong.

I set down the canvas and got up, fighting my fear. Evil hung thick in the air. Demons were in the house. I swallowed hard and approached Rachel's room with leaden legs. Getting closer, I heard small, muted sounds of whimpering. I opened the door and flipped on the overhead light. The room reflected an eerie state of nonchaos. Rachel was always very active, even in her sleep. For that reason, I expected her covers to be rumpled, with her scrunched up in the middle.

That's not what I found.

Her bed was perfect, like a soldier's bunk. The covers were straight and taut; the little yellow pillow in the exact center of the top of the bed. Instead of Rachel lying on it, a doll was in her place. Its plastic head was directly in the center of the pillow face up, and the covers tucked neatly beneath its chin. Nothing was out of place. The entire room was far neater than I had left it just thirty minutes ago when I had put Rachel to bed. In short, everything was wrong. And Rachel was nowhere to be seen.

Taking in the bizarre, *impossible* scenario, a chill sliced through me. No human hands had arranged the bed that way. Only a demon could have done that.

My eyes scanned the room for Rachel. I heard intermittent whimpers but couldn't tell where they came from. She obviously wasn't underneath the flat covers. I scanned the floor—no Rachel. I went to the far side of the bed, expecting to find her on the floor. She wasn't there. Panicked, I sprinted back to the other side and looked along the mattress, then checked the closet, thinking she had somehow gotten inside and shut the doors behind her. Nothing in there but her tiny shoes.

"Rachel!"

I heard her whimper again, this time louder. I tracked the sound. There, in the corner, stuffed in the ten-inch-by-ten-inch space between the wooden legs of the toy high chair, I saw her. She was rolled up like a pill bug in an impossibly small space and unable to move. Horrified, I ran to free her. It wasn't easy. I had to hold her with one hand while pulling the toy off with the other to slowly separate them and then gently uncurl her body. Her eyes blinked against the harsh overhead light, as if she had been asleep until that moment. She looked frightened and confused.

"Rachel, are you OK?" I cooed.

At my words, she burst into tears.

I pulled her close, letting her bury her face in my neck as I rubbed her back and massaged her limbs. When her cries lessened and muscles relaxed, I held her with my left arm, then lifted my right arm high with the fist clenched. "Satan!" I said firmly and fearlessly. "How dare you touch this child? In the name of Jesus, I command you to leave this room and this house! Flee this home and this family. In Jesus' name, I demand that you take your hands off this child and leave her alone! She's not yours! She belongs to God! Satan, leave this house and never come back. You are not welcome here!"

I stood quiet for a minute, comforting Rachel with soft pats and gentle kisses. Then I raised my right arm again, this time openhanded. "Father, thank You for not allowing the enemy to hurt her. Please send the Holy Spirit to comfort us and bring peace to this house. Post angels in this room tonight to stand guard over her as she sleeps. Don't let the demon molest her again. Keep her safe, Lord, and take away her fears. Watch over her. She is Your child. I know that You love her. Thank You, Father. In Jesus' name, amen."

The evil presence vanished, and peace took its place. I rocked Rachel back to sleep, put her back into bed, then left her door open so I would hear any movement or disturbance. All evening I thought about Hal's ominous warning: *Satan may go after your future children to get back at you.* Tonight it had come true. The battle lines had been drawn. Satan meant business, but so did I. He was out to destroy my precious little girl. I was determined to keep her safely in the arms of God. I knew this was just the beginning of a long, hard fight over this child whom I loved so much.

* * * * *

When Carl got home, I told him what happened.

"Is she OK? She didn't get bruised, did she?"

"She's fine, just scared."

"And you think a demon shoved her under the high chair?"

"Yes."

He wearily started to undress. "You have to admit, it sounds pretty farfetched. But with your history, who knows? Anyway, it's over, and I need sleep."

I wanted to convince him this was serious. We were supposed to be a team. I needed him to fight this battle with me. Instead, he doubted my story and acted detached, so I dropped it. From that point on, Satan's plan to destroy our family was on full throttle.

CHAPTER

11

The next two weeks played out like the Cold War: there were no more blowups, simply a settling of sorts—a silent, mutual acknowledgment of the wall separating us. My heart grew as hard as flint. Carl's grew dark as he realized I would never love him in return. We were both disillusioned by the ugliness at church. The dream that brought us to Idaho lay shattered at our feet.

But we still had responsibilities. Carl worked as hard as ever, while I did day care and taught Rachel to talk and sing her ABC's. Out of the blue, Babette sent a generous check with instructions to buy Rachel new dresses. This was sweet, but where would she wear them? Life existed between the four walls of home, which was now quieter after one of the cats jumped on Chester's cage and slit his throat with a sharp claw. Angry at the cats, I sent them back where they came from. Our home grew sadder and lonelier by the day.

One morning I called Gayle for help. "I need to clear my head, to figure things out. I can't stay with my parents, as Laura has the guesthouse. Can Rachel and I stay with you for a couple of weeks?"

"Of course, stay as long as you like."

"Thanks. You were right, Gayle; this marriage was a mistake."

"We all make them, Cheryl. It's part of life."

That night I told Carl. His face filled with pain. "How long will you be gone?"

"I don't know. Two weeks, maybe longer."

"Are you coming back?"

I didn't know.

*   *   *   *   *

February 14, 1980, dawned snowy and cold. Carl took the morning off so he could take us to the airport. When I went to make breakfast, a card and chocolates were on the table. Suddenly, I realized I was leaving on Valentine's Day. Somehow I had forgotten. The fact that *he* had remembered testified that our marriage was more than a little one sided.

Carl came in while I was reading the card; he had just showered and stood there in a towel. It reminded me of the night he had rescued me from the burglars. Other memories of our eleven months together flashed like a movie in my head: card games; reading in bed; driving to Yellowstone; and the many, many fights.

He stood there dripping; his eyes sad, searching mine for signs of hope. "I couldn't let you leave without showing you I still love you. I hope you'll come back."

I silently nodded. It was all so sad. But I couldn't wait to get back to California where I belonged. Would God ever forgive me for this? I hoped my faith would be renewed by returning to my old church where the members had always been warm and friendly. Would it be different now, returning as a failure at marriage? Gayle, Jim, and Pat would always be there for me. That was comforting. But they couldn't put my life back together. Surely, Satan would use this separation to swoop in fiercer than ever. That was a chilling thought. But no matter. My life in Idaho was a poison I had to vomit up to find relief.

When the plane took off, Rachel delighted in seeing clouds outside the window. She didn't know this was a major turning point in her life. To her, this was an adventure. Gazing at the heavens, I tried to look ahead with hope. I needed redemption and to learn how to live up to God's stern standards of Christian perfection without failing every other day, or every hour. If I did so, maybe God would let me find another husband; someone I could love passionately—the way married people are supposed to love each other.

The flight passed quickly. We would land soon. I stroked Rachel's sleek, black curls and dared to picture us with someone new, as part of a happy family. Then I realized that I could only remarry if my marriage ended because of adultery. As far as I knew, Carl had been as faithful as a cocker spaniel.

* * * * *

As expected, we were greeted that first Sabbath with excitement and warmth. Even so, I felt like Naomi when she returned to Israel with Ruth. I had left full, with a husband and a future. I returned with nothing. At the age of twenty-one, I was an empty, bitter woman.

After two weeks, I called Carl. "I've decided not to come back."

"I figured as much," he said. "It's not what I want, but I respect your decision."

He promised to bring my car and belongings a few weeks later. In the meantime, I looked for work and agreed to rent a bedroom from a couple at church. As the chains that bound me in Idaho fell away one by one, I failed to realize that Satan had new chains waiting for me—the chains of guilt and divorce.

Stella and Mel were longtime church members with one child still at home. Renting their small spare bedroom was a step down from owning my own home, but it was fine for the time being. I found work in a hospital nearby. With help from Mom, I bought an inexpensive used car for the interim.

At first, everything worked out amazingly well. Work was doable; and my landlords didn't challenge my faith, or so I thought. Little by little, their small, casual comments hit me. Stella remarked on the cut of my top, the length of my skirt, or the fit of my pants. Horizontal stripes on a snug top accentuated my modest bust; this was ungodly. Stella found I used too much makeup, though she conceded that, in her opinion, none at all was best. Her comments escalated whenever Mel would pay me a compliment or stare a little too long in her presence.

Because I already felt like a harlot for leaving Carl without just cause, Stella's cutting words not only hurt but often felt justified. I started questioning my own judgement of how I looked, and pretty soon, guilt-driven legalism kicked in full force. I toned down my appearance using Stella's measure of Christian modesty until friends such as Hal and Beth said I was starting to look very "Adventist." Their observation wasn't complimentary; but feeling a strange sense of pride, I was glad I could at least look the part of the perfect Adventist woman on the outside until I became perfect on the inside as well, despite my fall from grace.

About that time, several young adults around my age started attending church, including Sean and his engaged friends Antonio and Lily. We quickly became close friends and did everything at church together, including attending potlucks, game nights, and Wednesday night prayer meetings.

One night Sean and Antonio surprised me by coming over while Stella and Mel were out with their daughter. They brought Mark with them—a young man they had ministered to that afternoon in Hollywood. Happy for their company, I made hot tea and served cookies, which Rachel was happy to share with us. Mark was thin, unkempt, hungry, and very likely high on something; but he was sweet and very interested in hearing more about God. We all did our best to make him feel comfortable and accepted.

Time flew by and before we knew it, Mel and Stella came walking through the door. We all smiled in welcome and offered them tea and cookies too. To my surprise, Stella gave me a hard look; her mouth was a straight line of dignified unfriendliness. It was late, she said. It was time for everyone to go home. I was confused and embarrassed at her rudeness. The boys, looking embarrassed too, left quickly saying Thank you on the way out. Sean said he would take Mark home with him for a shower and a good night's sleep and would bring him to church the following Sabbath.

When they were gone, I asked Stella why she was angry. Mel and their daughter had already excused themselves and gone to bed, eager to avert the storm.

"Cheryl, this simply cannot happen again, or we will be forced to ask you to move."

"Why? What did I do? What can't happen again?"

"Cheryl, you allowed *gentlemen callers* inside our home when we were not here." At my look of confusion, she added, "You were alone—unchaperoned! Can't you see how inappropriate that is? What kind of example does that set for our child? Whether you see the problem or not, that will not be tolerated in this household. Do you understand?"

There was no reasoning with her. It was her house, not mine.

"Of course," I acquiesced. "It will never happen again."

That night I lay in bed and tried to see her side of things, but I could not. Antonio and Sean were trying to save an addict's life through loving Christian hospitality. They had come to me for help, and I had given it freely without hesitation. Surely offering tea and cookies to a hungry man was a good thing in God's eyes. Knowing I had already turned myself inside out to suit Stella's standards, I realized it was time to find my own place. I was not a child. I could make my own decisions about Christian deportment. I still yearned for a level of perfection that would please God and secure my salvation, but I did not need others constantly pointing out my shortcomings along the way. The next day I went apartment hunting.

* * * * *

I quickly found a spacious one-bedroom apartment in Reseda for the two of us. I had no furniture, so we made do with an old mattress on the floor for me and a pile of soft blankets for Rachel. It felt like camping, but at least there was no tension or fighting. I continued working at the hospital until my old temp agency offered a better full-time job in the defense industry. Since the hours were longer, I moved Rachel to full-time day care with Penny, a sweet mom whose own kids were nearly grown. Penny watched a dozen toddlers in her lovely hillside home. Rachel was very happy there.

Several weeks later, Carl brought my things. He had found a home for Boofa and left Rebo with a friend. It was now spring, and the weather was turning warm. Since there was no real animosity between us, Carl stayed with us for several days before heading back.

On Sunday afternoon, we all went to the pool in my apartment complex to cool off. Rachel played on the pool steps, wearing her pool wings, while Carl and I dangled our feet in the water and talked.

"Thanks for hauling everything back," I said, and meant it. "But I've looked through all the boxes, and my mother's gold jewelry is missing. Do you know where it is? Is it possible you forgot to pack it?"

He blushed and turned away. "Everything got packed; nothing of yours is left in the house."

"Then where is it? I know I rarely wear it anymore, but it meant a lot to me."

His embarrassment grew more acute. "I know. Um, do you remember Tiffany? From AA?"

"Yes. You never liked her much. Why?"

"About a week after you left, she started coming over. A lot. In fact, she pretty much moved in."

My feet froze midsplash. The world seemed to pause and shift on its axis.

"You *slept* with her?"

He blushed more and nodded.

"Carl, a *week?* How could you do that with someone you never even liked?"

He shrugged. "I knew you weren't coming back. I was hurting. She was there. End of story."

His news was shocking. Even more surprising was that it didn't hurt—not really. My pride was wounded but not my heart. In fact, I quickly focused on the fact that his adultery had freed me to move on.

I offered a sad smile of regret for the mess our lives had become.

"I'm sorry," he said.

"Me too. But wait, what does Tiffany have to do with my mother's jewelry?"

"She packed your things. If you're missing stuff, she must have helped herself."

Ouch. Ironically, the idea of her stealing my treasures stung more than her indiscretion with Carl.

*   *   *   *   *

On his last night with us, Carl and I tied up loose ends, deciding what to do with the house and how to divvy up our debts. It was a painful process. We both felt like failures and worried how our mistakes would affect Rachel. The next day he left for Idaho, leaving me to face life in Los Angeles as a single mom again.

Life after that fell into a routine. I liked being independent, but it wasn't easy. On many nights, police helicopters circled overhead, chasing criminals in the empty lot behind my unit. One evening a man claiming to be from the Census Bureau tried to shake open my door before finally giving up. And it was tough paying the rent on what I earned. Satan was tightening the noose.

As soon as Laura moved out of the guesthouse, I moved back in. Living there saved money. It also increased the number of demonic attacks. Rachel started crying more, and it was hard to know why. She could have missed Carl, was tired from getting up earlier for the longer commute, could have experienced anxiety from our frequent moves, or it could have been the presence of demons. Likewise, my own anxiety went up for the same reasons. It was harder to fight off demons when I was too tired to see straight, and Satan knew that. All in all, I felt trapped again. I didn't really want to live there, but it was all I could afford. So I stayed.

On the plus side, Rachel was seeing more of my parents. They enjoyed getting to know her and delighted in her progress. On one occasion, Dad excitedly pointed out that Rachel had come up with a new way to do her puzzle. Apparently, it was too easy using the picture, so she turned all the pieces over—cardboard side up—and put it together using just the shapes.

"She's only eighteen months old!" he said in amazement. "At that age, she must be very smart to figure out how to make a puzzle more challenging!"

And so our lives went, finding the positives where we could.

Eventually, Carl sold the house and repaid our parents. Then he surprised everyone by moving back to Los Angeles to work for my brother Tom's father-in-law. He saw Rachel when he could. To please Babette, the three of us spent that next Thanksgiving at Carl's aunt's house. Babette said she was sure we would work out our differences and reconcile. It was fun to see everyone, and I wished things were different. But my heart hadn't changed. We would never be a family again. Satan had won that battle.

In December, I worked two jobs to earn money for a retainer. Soon I had enough to file for divorce. Carl hadn't adopted Rachel and didn't fight for custody. I didn't seek child support or alimony. We broke even on the house, leaving no assets to divide. Everything was amicable. In fact, we stayed such good friends that when Tom and Cindy had a birthday party for their son Kyle, Carl came too.

The party was held two-hours' drive away, near the air force base where Tom was stationed. It was a casual party, with just a few friends and neighbors, plus a handful of kids. We spent the afternoon visiting in the front yard while Tom barbecued hamburgers.

Among the guests, one guy stood out—Matt—one of Tom's coworkers on base. He had short, light-brown hair and wore scuffed cowboy boots, tight-fitting jeans, and a well-worn straw cowboy hat. He was gorgeous and knew it. All afternoon I tried to ignore his overt attention, but it was a challenge.

When it got dark, Carl stood up. "We need to get back. I work in the morning," he explained.

Cindy looked disappointed.

"Carl, there's a big dance on base tonight. We already lined up a babysitter. Can't you guys spend the night and leave early tomorrow?"

"Cindy, your dad expects me to be to work on time. I need a good night's sleep." He glanced over and immediately read my own disappointment. "Cheryl, you don't have to be back until Sunday night. I can drive back alone if you can find a ride home tomorrow."

Matt adjusted his hat and looked my way. "My girlfriend and her sister are driving to Los Angeles tomorrow. They have room." His girlfriend was not at the party and would not be going to the dance.

I felt torn.

"It's up to you, Cheryl," Carl plaintively interjected.

Our divorce wasn't final, and it was simply good manners to leave a party with the person you came with. Even so, temptation burned in me. We weren't a couple anymore. I wanted to go dancing.

"I'll stay," I said, trying to sound nonchalant.

Hurt and betrayal filled Carl's eyes. Pulling dignity around him like a cloak, he nodded. "I'll get Rachel's car seat." He went to the car alone while the rest of us looked on.

Somewhere in that exchange, I had switched sides. I wasn't on Carl's team anymore. It stung for a second, then a delicious sense of freedom took over. I dismissed Carl's disapproval and tuned out God's.

The dance hall was dark and pulsated with rock music. I danced with several airmen, including Matt. When it was time for a break, I found our group at the bar. Every chair was taken.

Matt patted his lap. "Sit. I won't bite."

Warning bells sounded. The Holy Spirit said No. The enemy pushed me to give in to Matt's flirting. Meanwhile, my back started hurting as it always did when I was due to start my monthly cycle.

"OK," I said. "Just for a minute." I sat lightly on his knees.

"Thirsty?" he asked. "I just opened this beer. I can get another one."

I hesitated at the edge of the cliff. Trying to be perfect had gotten me nowhere, I reasoned. I reached for the brown bottle.

"Cheryl, are you sure you want that?" Tom's somewhat mocking question was in fact a parachute—a chance to resist the devil. Tom knew I had been sober for more than two years. I met his eyes with a smile. "I'm sure. My back hurts. This will help. It'll be fine."

"OK, up to you," he said. Just like that, the lifeline fell out of reach.

I tipped the bottle and took a long drink, feeling a rush of sharp condemnation as the liquid burned its way down to my stomach, which was followed by euphoria surging through my veins. The deed was done and could not be undone. I was not sober anymore. I drank with gusto until it was gone. Satan's delight at my folly was palpable, driving me to the dance floor with Matt in tow, Carl forgotten.

CHAPTER

12

After that weekend, I started dating men from work and slipped back into old habits. That first beer opened the door to more drinking and allowed other morals to fall by the wayside. I avoided AA meetings but went to church, though not regularly. Faith took a back seat while Evil crept closer. I felt powerless to stop. Satan was having his way.

At the same time, my health went downhill. My menstrual cycles grew longer and more painful; a condition aggravated by my job. Lifting supplies and sitting for long hours at the drafting table while repairing schematics was painful. Something was wrong. By June, I felt bad enough to require time off with worker's comp. I rested a lot, hoping the pain would go away.

During that summer hiatus, I visited Tom and Cindy at the base. That first night I tagged along to watch Tom and his coworkers—including Matt—play softball. He was in the outfield, watching me as he played. I wondered if he still had that same girlfriend.

After an hour, I got too sleepy to stay. It had been a long day, and I was hurting. I left Rachel with Cindy to play with her cousin Kyle and went back to their bungalow. Pretty soon, I was happily watching TV on the couch. Suddenly, the doorbell rang.

It was Matt. He had wine and flowers and looked hopeful.

"Hello," I said with surprise.

"Hi. I'm Matt. Remember?"

I nodded.

"I asked Tom if I could call on you."

"I thought you had a girlfriend."

"We broke up last month."

I stepped back to let him inside.

We spent the evening getting to know each other; the family eventually joined us. Matt was handsome, funny, charming, sensitive, and intelligent. We shared an instant attraction that grew as the hours flew by. It felt as though we were the only two people in the room.

All that week we spent every free minute together. We went to dinner, the movies, swimming, and miniature golfing. He hung out at the house and joined us for meals. By the end of my stay, we were a couple. I hated to leave, but we all had to get back to our normal routines.

Back home there were doctors' visits and more tests. When weeks of rest made no difference, I quit my job. I needed laparoscopic surgery but had no insurance, so my parents paid for it. The surgeon found the problem and fixed it but said the condition was chronic and would likely come back. For the moment, though, I was pain free.

All summer Matt and I talked and saw each other often. Our romance was intoxicating—a wild ride of adventurous stolen moments. With little resistance, I adapted to his lifestyle, partying and smoking right along with him. Church fell completely away. I was smitten enough to turn a blind eye to all the potential problems with our romance, including his temper, which was as quick as his wit.

In August, my divorce went through. Matt proposed in September, then took us to meet his family. All went well until the drive home. That's when I made the mistake of saying something negative about Matt's friend. In an instant, the relaxed atmosphere in the car exploded as he gave full vent to his anger. He yelled loud enough to wake Rachel, who had been sleeping in the back seat. He pounded the steering wheel, cursed a blue streak, and threatened to call off the wedding.

"How dare you say that? I've known him all my life," he said, glaring through the darkness. "That's longer than I've known you! If I had to choose, who do you think I'd pick? Not you! Just think about that." He stewed for a minute and then went on. "If you want to call off the wedding, just say so. We can end it, here and now!" Another pause. "Well? What's it going to be? Do you want to marry me or not?"

I was hurt and shaken to the core. I knew I should end it, repent, and let God lead me back to a place of grace and redemption. But it felt too late. I was in too deep. I needed a man in my life and couldn't risk losing Matt. The enemy had me convinced that I had been an unloving wife to Carl, a marginal church member, and was now a twenty-something single mother with dwindling prospects. How could all my dreams of love and happiness be suddenly, inexplicably, slipping out of reach? I had to do something.

"Of course, I want to marry you," I whispered, trying to regain equilibrium. "Just lower your voice, please; you're scaring Rachel."

His eyes shot to the rearview mirror. There was Rachel, watching this awful drama in wide-eyed silence. He cleared his throat, regaining control.

"Well OK, then," he said, quieter than before. "Just don't insult my friends, that's all. Promise me that, and we'll forget this ever happened."

"I promise," I said quietly.

He reached over and took my hand. We rode like that for many miles while I pondered the cost of selling my soul.

* * * * *

We married in December, less than a year after meeting at the birthday party. We moved into a two-bedroom apartment close to the base. Matt's coworker Clint managed the building as a side job and lived on-site with his wife, Trish, who quickly became a good friend.

Those first few months of marriage were happy ones for the most part. Matt and I tried learning how to play tennis together while he also learned the game of golf from Tom; Matt taught me how to play backgammon, and we enjoyed playing board games together; we went dancing; he left me romantic notes; I cooked him lavish meals. On the practical side, I went back to school, taking classes at the local junior college while Rachel attended preschool on the base.

That spring Matt said he wanted a son, preferably before he left the air force. Before the pregnancy was confirmed, I was given a round of antibiotics known to cause birth defects, which God impressed me to stop taking. Then early in the pregnancy, I was inadvertently exposed to measles. Both incidents made me wonder if this child was under attack from conception. Not taking any chances, I quit smoking and drinking alcohol and coffee.

Unfortunately, Matt's party habits continued which gradually dimmed our initial honeymoon-period of happiness. His drinking escalated, and nearly caused a disaster. After a night of barhopping with Clint, he came home late to find me playing cards with Trish in their apartment. It angered him that I wasn't at home to greet him; so when I asked him to carry a sleeping Rachel home, he got belligerent.

"Do it yourself. Let's go. I'm tired."

He was too drunk to argue with, so I scooped up Rachel and staggered down the walkway to our apartment. She was sound asleep and therefore essentially dead weight. Pain seared my uterus as I prayed I wouldn't drop her before he unlocked the stubborn door. I was up all night spotting and cramping, certain I was losing the baby as punishment for going back to the world. The accusing voices taunted and ridiculed, pushing me to make a promise to God that things would be different. I would find my way back to Him somehow. Finally, morning came. The cramps stopped with the dawn—I was still pregnant.

Despite all the early drama and scares, the following March—two weeks past due—Nick was born, big, strong, and healthy. We had dodged all the bullets. I was grateful! Our family was complete. Naturally, everything revolved around the baby. I was breastfeeding, so I abstained from anything unhealthy. After several weeks, though, I realized he wasn't getting enough milk. Not understanding that I could do both, I switched to bottle-feeding. Gone was my reason to say No to alcohol and cigarettes. I could indulge in anything as long as I was willing to endure guilt when the Holy Spirit pricked my conscience, which became increasingly hard to do. That's when the battle between Matt's freewheeling lifestyle and God's unwavering principles got heated. I finally came to a point where I needed to pick one or the other.

Unsurprisingly, I slid back to Matt's side, forgetting prayerful promises and the miracle of a healthy baby with no defects. It was a step backward, but I never really reverted all the way to the old me. I still needed Matt's approval, but I changed in other ways. Worldly entertainment wasn't fun anymore. It once more left me uncomfortable. I also became more vulnerable than ever to demonic attacks. In response, I stopped turning a blind eye and resented how the vices of the world had taken over our marriage. As a result, I lashed out when Matt overindulged, which he didn't appreciate. Escalating fights ensued, fed by his petty jealousies and my critical nitpicking. We still loved each other; but our relationship was fire and ice, with the kids in the middle.

When Matt got close to leaving the air force, he ordered me to find temporary work in Los Angeles where the pay was higher. Nick was only six weeks old. I begged him to figure out another way to build a financial safety net. He wouldn't budge. With a broken heart, I stayed with my parents and found work while Matt stayed home with the kids, putting them in the base's day care when he worked. All day I worked, drawing schematics while chain-smoking and drinking coffee, crying often. I was a mess. After three weeks, I quit before they could fire me. Matt took me home, and we started planning our move back to civilian life.

Tom and Matt had taken the Federal Aviation Administration's (FAA) test to be air traffic controllers. Both passed, hoping for jobs in California.

After President Reagan's mass firing of FAA controllers who had gone on strike, the available jobs in California filled up first. By the time Matt was discharged, he had to go on a waiting list. That left us with no choice but to move back to Matt's hometown north of Los Angeles to wait for an opening outside California.

Not knowing how long we would be there, we squeezed into a three-bedroom house with Matt's dad, stepmom, their new baby, and her two teenagers. For work, Matt picked grapes, and I designed newspaper ads at night, while Rachel started kindergarten at the public school that was on a year-round schedule. For fun, we went on long bike rides, explored different parks, and I taught Rachel to read. It was a waiting game.

The enemy was right there, too, filling Matt's head with doubts and fears that he would never get hired or be able to provide for us. When pressures mounted, Matt took our arguments somewhere private, so others wouldn't hear his cruel words or see him get physical. I knew it was the fear talking, but it hurt deeply.

When the grape-picking season was over, Matt went to the lake to help my dad trim trees and clean up the hillside behind the house. Dad paid Matt for his time, which was a blessing. But he also stirred up trouble, letting me know that Matt went to see my old friend Julie in the valley and didn't come home until the next morning. Matt tried but couldn't convince Dad of his innocence. For some reason, Matt's temper got worse after that; he even left a hand-shaped bruise on my arm during one argument. We needed a miracle.

Shortly after my birthday in September, the miracle came. Matt got hired in Texas. It wasn't where we wanted to live, but we went where the work was. His first stop was training school in Oklahoma for three months. I stayed with his family and kept working. During that time, a deep loneliness set in that I chalked up to missing Matt. Despite our troubles, I missed him deeply. He had become my world.

In January, we packed up all our belongings and left California with high hopes and borrowed cash from my mom, heading to a completely new adventure. We found a cheap two-bedroom apartment in a neighborhood known for its outstanding school district. We put Rachel in kindergarten at the public school. We made friends in the complex and at Matt's work. We began a new life.

On the one hand, everything was fresh and exciting, with fun challenges and a whole new environment. On the other, it was lonely living so far from friends and family. Matt felt the same way but was too busy learning his job to dwell on it. He had arrived with several other trainees from Oklahoma. Matt sailed through one test after another, leaning on his four years of being an air traffic controller in the air force. His fellow trainees had no military experience, and many failed. As more friends left, Matt's concerns over his own tenure built up like a simmering volcano, which matched the volatile Texas weather. One storm we experienced turned the sky an eerie green before a lightning bolt split a tree outside our living-room window.

We also had to live on a trainee's paycheck. For the entire first year, we lived on a shoestring budget. As in Idaho, I had to make do with inexpensive fun. We found a library; I became friends with a neighbor who was an artist like me; and the kids made friends in the complex. We got by, but the loss I had felt when Matt was in Oklahoma lingered like smoke from a fire, permeating heart and soul.

One day I looked out the window, searching the sky for answers.

"What is it, God? What's causing this ache that won't go away?"

"Me," came His undeniable answer.

I had only attended church a handful of times since marrying Matt. Now we were in Baptist country; I hadn't seen a single Seventh-day Adventist church in our area. So I reached for the Bible and tried to reconnect. The aroma of His presence was faintly alluring, close but not close enough. I needed more. Pushing away my doubts, I prayed for a way back.

The door opened just days later.

* * * * *

Nick and I were walking Rachel home from the school bus stop when our neighbor waved me over. A nearby community church was having a free Easter egg hunt. She wanted us to go with her family.

"It's this Saturday at eleven in the morning," she said. "Let's get there early; there'll be a crowd!"

When we got there, the lawn behind the church was filling up fast. Our two families joined the crowd of parents and kids. Up front, a tall man was trying to get everyone's attention.

"We'll start the Easter egg hunt in just a minute," he said in a stage whisper. "But first we need to do a little housekeeping." He pointed to the church. A large stained-glass window faced the lawn and the woods beyond that. "Another church rents our building every Saturday. They're starting services right now, so everyone keep your voices low so we don't disturb them, OK?" He looked around, making sure everyone was in agreement. Then someone in a rabbit suit sauntered around the corner and waved at the kids, making Rachel jump with excitement.

"OK, kids," the first man said. "Go find those eggs!"

While Rachel took off and Matt led Nick by the hand to find eggs, I looked back at the church window with a thrill of excitement. Only one denomination held church services at 11:00 A.M. on a Saturday. It had to be mine! I quickly took pictures of the Easter Bunny and the kids finding eggs, then went over to Matt and took hold of his arm.

"Hon, I'll explain later, but I've got to go. I'm going inside for the church service. Please take the kids home when they're done, then come back for me in an hour."

I expected questions, or at least a hard time. I got neither. He just furrowed his brow in slight confusion and then nodded.

"Thanks. I'll fix lunch when we're all home. See you in an hour."

Inside, the vestibule was empty and quiet. I carefully opened the inner door and sat in a back pew. The stained-glass window I had noted from outside was behind the pulpit, beautifully lit with the morning sun. The children's story had just started. As I sat there, something inside clicked gently, yet firmly into place. I was back home, and it felt very good. The gaping God-shaped hole of loneliness that had bothered me from California to Texas began to fill with the presence of God.

* * * * *

"You're off tomorrow, right?" I asked Matt over breakfast.

"Yeah. Why?"

"You're working tonight and you'll be tired in the morning, but I thought you might like to go with us to church."

He glanced up briefly and shrugged. "I was planning to hit a few golf balls in the morning, but I can do it after lunch."

I had been attending church for weeks, but this was the first time I had invited him. I was elated at his response but didn't make a fuss. I didn't want him changing his mind. After that, he joined us more often than not, giving us the chance to get acquainted with church members as a family. It was a definite step forward toward faith for us all. So of course, Satan attacked us at home.

As our church attendance increased, Matt's moods swung unpredictably between attempted piety and fierce anger, more so when he was stressed or had too much to drink. One particular Sabbath was especially bad, making me question if church was worth the chaos that so often followed.

We had just gotten home from church. The kids were playing outside on the patio. I was making sandwiches while Matt poured drinks. My mind drifted as I spread mayonnaise on bread, thinking about the previous week. Without meaning to, I let out a sigh. Suddenly, Matt slammed his fist on the counter.

"What?" he demanded angrily. "What's wrong now?"

Startled, I blinked at him. "Nothing; it was just a sigh. It didn't mean anything."

"Yes, it did! You're never satisfied. What will it take to make you happy?"

I should have taken a breath and remained calm. Instead, I lashed out as I had done since childhood. Abuse and discord had always been a part of life for me, including inappropriate touching and physical abuse—getting burned by a cigarette and being chased with a knife. Now my heated retort spun the situation out of control. Angry beyond reason, Matt picked me up by my upper arms and shook me like a rag doll. I could see the kids watching us through the patio window, looking frightened.

"Matt, stop! The kids—you're scaring them."

He immediately dropped me but was still angry.

"Yeah, well, it's your fault I get so mad. You never know when to quit."

I needed to cry, to break down, and to regroup. But there wasn't time. The kids needed reassurance and lunch. So I let it go and went on. It was obvious Satan wouldn't let go quietly, but that didn't stop me from feeling defensive and distrustful of Matt's mercurial love.

Beyond our internal struggles, other dramas played out in our apartment complex that made me feel unsafe. A couple next door fought violently. A drug dealer several doors down got attacked with a knife. The playground had dirty needles everywhere. Then one day Rachel came back from playing outside with Nick to say a man had tried to lure them into his truck. Even a family walk to a nearby park almost turned deadly when Rachel took off running, right into the path of a speeding car. It missed her by inches. In response, I grew sterner and made more rules to keep everyone safe, while Matt stewed about work, our finances, and his own struggle with faith.

Not satisfied with making us feel unsafe, Satan's next ploy was to steal Rachel's happiness. It was now late spring, with less than a month left of school. Rachel loved school, but we all looked forward to summer. On a sunny day after school, the next blow fell.

"Here, Mommy," Rachel said while handing over a note. "It's from my teacher. Can I have a snack?"

"Just an apple. We're eating dinner early so Daddy can go to work."

While the kids washed up, I read the note, then went to find Matt in the bedroom.

"Look!" I shrieked, waving the note at him. "Rachel can't attend kindergarten anymore!"

He looked confused. "What? Let me see." He took it and read for himself. "This says she's not old enough for kindergarten. Her birthday comes too late in the fall."

"I don't understand. Why didn't they tell us that when we registered her in January? The school year is almost over!" She had already had eleven months of school and could out read her classmates.

He sat on the bed, looking defeated. "We can't change the law."

The next day I walked Rachel past her classroom to the administration's desk. It was story time, and Rachel was missing out. "Mommy, did I do something wrong? I want to go to school!" She tried to pull me toward her classroom.

"No, Rachel, you didn't do anything wrong."

"Then why don't they want me?" She started to cry as we continued walking away from her friends and beloved teacher. My heart broke as I signed her out and collected the treasures they had removed from her cubby. It would be a long wait for fall.

* * * * *

In the midst of our stormy sea, the tide turned at last. Pastor Chuck approached us after church. He was single, friendly, and close to our age. He was our only pastor, and we liked him and his sermons.

"Hello, Matt and Cheryl," Pastor Chuck said. "I'd like to talk to you about something important. Could I stop by your place later today?"

Matt hesitated. He had planned on a nap after lunch. Then he gave Chuck an apologetic smile. "Sure, come anytime. We're right up the road."

Again, I didn't make a fuss but couldn't hide my happiness. This was an answer to prayer!

The pastor came after lunch while the kids napped. We sat in the living room and drank soda.

"Matt, I noticed you've been coming to church with Cheryl," he said. Matt nodded uncomfortably.

"I want you to know your family has made a wonderful addition to our congregation," he said, smiling encouragingly.

"Thanks," Matt said.

"Yes, well, you're probably wondering what this is leading up to."

We nodded.

"Cheryl told me she was baptized and had Rachel dedicated in California. Matt, since you're now coming, too, I thought you might want to take Bible studies with me. What do you think?"

Matt shot me a questioning look.

I shook my head and shrugged. I was as surprised as he was.

"I hadn't really thought about it."

Pastor Chuck nodded his understanding. "Don't think of it as a big commitment. You're not agreeing to join the church or anything. This is just our way of helping you to get to know God and learn more about our denomination."

Matt said nothing.

The pastor cleared his throat and sat up straighter. "If you like, I could come here. We'd do one lesson a week. What do you say?"

Matt rubbed the seam of his jeans, with his eyes on the floor, then looked up. "I guess we can try it; see how it goes. I'm not making any promises, though."

"That's fine!" the pastor said, beaming. "We'll start next week."

After the pastor left, Matt eyed me suspiciously. "Did you have anything to do with this?"

"No. He never said anything to me about Bible study." That satisfied him.

* * * * *

The first night of the Bible study, we ate dinner early, so the kids would be in bed when the pastor arrived. I stayed to listen while Chuck led Matt through verses and questions, but they barely noticed my presence. I wasn't needed, so the next week I got busy in another room. I heard them talking in serious tones one minute, then laughing over a discussion point the next. They were hitting it off.

From week to week, I saw Matt's countenance change. His smile came more readily. He relaxed more and played with the kids more often. Patience became more the rule than the exception. Conversely, his anger took longer to erupt and evaporated more quickly. Even his stops at the bar after work tapered off some, making evenings more enjoyable.

The biggest change came when the guys from church invited Matt to play touch football at the park. Matt didn't make friends easily, so it surprised me when he agreed to play. Both sides gave it all they had; no one held back. Even so, it made everyone laugh good-naturedly when Matt missed a play or fumbled the ball and let out a curse word and blushed at his own faux pas. More than once, Chuck or one of the others would thump him on the back and say it was no big deal. I watched from the sidelines with the other wives, amazed to see the man he was becoming. Prayers were being answered. My heart's desires were coming true.

But as so often happens, this amazing spiritual victory coincided with a setback. This time it was on my side. I found myself struggling daily to tame my tongue with the kids, especially Rachel. My need for perfection and control often crashed headlong with her untamed zest for exploration and uncontainable energy. Tears often resulted on both sides, leaving Nick fretful and Matt dumbfounded regarding how to help. I frequently felt like a failure. The harder I worked for order, the more chaos prevailed.

Satan, the master puppeteer, had us by the strings. Blatant demonic attacks were rare, but our daily lives had his fingerprints all over them, right down to the pests that had plagued us since moving to Texas. We were bombarded by crawling and flying roaches, scabies, fire ants, and ringworm from Candy, a stray kitten that we had taken in. It was a rough season. And then a real storm hit.

* * * * *

"What do you mean you're quitting?" Matt asked Pastor Chuck. They had just started their study. Matt sounded hurt, and his tone had a nasty edge he usually reserved for me. "Pastors don't just up and quit! What happened? Why are you leaving?"

I dropped what I was doing to join them.

"Your pastor is leaving the church," Matt said accusingly. "He's moving back to his home state."

I was stunned. "Not right away, I hope. You and Matt are only halfway done."

The pastor looked embarrassed. "I'm moving at the end of the month. This will be our last lesson together."

He went on to explain that he felt called to be a lawyer, but the conference wouldn't allow him to attend law school and stay on as a pastor. When forced to pick a side, he chose law. "I hate doing this to the congregation—and you, Matt. But I'm certain this is my calling, and I must answer it."

"But what about me?" Matt asked, revealing his intense disappointment.

In that moment, it hit me just how important these lessons and Chuck's friendship had become to Matt. He sounded bereft, and I didn't blame him a bit. Chuck's sudden departure left Matt adrift and unprepared and our small church without a pastor.

"It's not fair!" Matt said. "They should never have made you choose."

"I agree," Chuck said. "But I have to respect their decision and follow my heart. If you like, one of the elders could take you through the rest of the lessons. I know you and Mike have gotten to be friends. Perhaps he'd make a good replacement if he has time. Shall I ask him for you?"

"I don't know," Matt sighed. "I'll think about it."

"Well, I'm here now. What do you say? One last lesson for the road?"

Matt tried to smile. "Sure. Why not?"

Before he left Texas, Chuck performed one last ritual for our family: he dedicated Nick. Then, just like that, he was gone, leaving a gaping, bleeding wound. Matt still attended church but just as often skipped services in favor of other distractions. His reaction was easy to understand but hard to live with. He blamed God for the entire debacle and responded accordingly, with a cold shoulder.

*   *   *   *   *

At the end of that extra-long summer, Matt and I discussed Rachel's schooling. We didn't think repeating kindergarten was necessary, so I told Matt that Gretchen, a woman at church who was the Adventist elementary school's secretary, had volunteered to take Rachel to the Adventist school downtown.

"That school will let her be in first grade," I said.

"I'd have to take her to school before work. My day shift starts at 7:00 a.m. Do they offer day care before school?"

"No, but Gretchen said you could drop Rachel at her house when you work early. Rachel can ride to school with Gretchen and her kids."

"I don't think it's a good idea, but we can try it. If it doesn't work out, we'll put her back in kindergarten at the public school."

The plan worked fine at first. Then the grueling routine started wearing on everyone, especially Rachel. Each day it got harder to wake her up. Her excitement wore off, then sullenness set in.

Near the end of the third week, Rachel refused to get into her pajamas. "Stop fussing, Rachel. You have school tomorrow."

She pushed my hand away. "I don't want to go to school."

"Why? I thought you liked school. Your teacher is nice, and you have friends there, right?"

"I don't care!" she wailed. "I don't like getting up in the dark."

I pulled her into my lap. "I know it's hard getting up early. Is that the only reason?"

"I don't like Ms. Gretchen."

This was a surprise. Gretchen was so nice at church. "Did something happen?"

"She makes us get in a circle in her living room every morning before we go to school."

"Are you praying?"

"No. She makes us say things over and over; and sometimes she yells, and it scares me."

That didn't sound like morning prayers. "What else does she do?"

"She lights candles and talks about spirits."

A chill shot through me. It was bad enough that Rachel was exhausted. Now she was being forced to participate with rituals that sounded like witchcraft. "OK. You don't have to go tomorrow. Daddy and I will figure something out. Let's get these pajamas on. It's time for bed."

Rachel went back to the public school kindergarten with the same teacher and classroom as before, just different classmates. The morning tears and complaints disappeared. She loved kindergarten and fit right in.

When I confronted Gretchen, she got angry and defensive. "I don't see what the big deal is. We weren't hurting her. You're the one who wanted her there. I was only trying to help."

CHAPTER

13

all flew by as Nick grew in leaps and bounds; Rachel enjoyed her extra round of kindergarten; they shared a case of chicken pox; and Matt hung in there while more trainees dropped out. Because he had no seniority, he worked many graveyard and double shifts. When he got time off, he often used alcohol to de-stress, so the kids and I learned to walk on eggshells to keep the peace. To appease me, Matt bought a drafting table so I could paint and let the kids and me pick out a puppy we named Tisha.

In January, our lease ended. We were eager to escape the roaches and unsavory atmosphere of the apartment complex. Matt had received a raise after completing the first level of training, which allowed us to find something better. At that time, housing was plentiful in Texas and the prices were low. We rented a nearly new three-bedroom, two-bathroom house in the same school district so Rachel wouldn't change schools.

A week before moving Matt left for a weekend of training in Oklahoma. While he was gone, I got busy cleaning out our bedroom closet. While in the process of sorting, I tried on several outfits that Friday afternoon, unaware that a small, shy critter lurked in one of the shirts.

The next day we joined our friends Kathy and Mike at their house for Sabbath lunch. Kathy and I were in the kitchen talking when she stopped what she was doing and pointed to my right arm.

"Cheryl, how long has that been there?"

I looked down and saw a tiny puncture wound in the crook of my arm and a bright-red streak running from the wound up along the vein for six or seven inches, heading straight for my heart. It didn't hurt, and I hadn't noticed it before. Kathy, who was a nurse, asked if I had been cleaning out woodpiles or rummaging in clothes that hadn't been worn in a while. I said I had been trying on clothes. Looking closer, she said it was a spider bite.

"Did you feel the spider bite you? Did it hurt?"

"No. I never felt a thing."

"When you tried on the clothes, were you bending your arms to see if they fit?"

At my nod, she sighed with sudden clarity. "It must have been a brown recluse. They're very common in this part of Texas."

She explained that a brown recluse spider's bite could lead to skin ulcerations and decayed flesh—nasty stuff. Thankfully, she knew just what to do. She called a doctor friend and asked him to call in an antibiotic for me that day. Then she pulled out a bag of medicinal charcoal pellets and melted them down in a pan on the stove. She liberally smeared the warm black poultice on the bite and the red streak, then wrapped my arm in foil and plastic wrap.

"Leave that on for three days. I'll hurry and make lunch so you can get your meds and go home. You basically have blood poisoning, so in a few hours you won't feel very good. But the charcoal will suck out the poison, and the antibiotics will take care of the rest. You'll be fine."

"Wow! It's a good thing I came over today," I marveled.

"Yes, God blessed you today, for sure!"

As predicted, I felt sick that night. But when I removed the poultice several days later, the red streak was gone and the wound had healed. It was a miracle.

* * * * *

The new house was surrounded by woods. It had a fireplace, a yard for Tisha, and an unusual glass atrium in the center of the home with floor-to-ceiling windows. The school bus stopped right out front, which was perfect for Rachel. There was even a community pool where she could take swimming lessons.

That summer my parents flew us out to California for a visit. We saw old friends, went to Disneyland with my sister Ellen and her family, hit the beach, fished, and enjoyed barbecues on the sundeck. It was a nice break, but Matt remained moody and stewed about work. The quarreling continued, even on vacation.

One afternoon I left him with the kids and escaped to a noon AA meeting. There I ran into Ellie and her son Kurt, who was now sober. After the meeting, Ellie told me an amazing story. She and a friend had decided to burn the family Ouija board.

"It was so strange," Ellie said, remembering. "That thing just wouldn't catch fire, even though it sat in a stack of burning logs! My friend and I were sitting on the couch watching it, when all of a sudden the board broke in two and a big ball of fire came out of it, flying across the room, right over our heads!" At my widening eyes, she leaned over and lowered her voice. "At the *exact* moment that board broke, Julie let out a blood-curdling scream from her bedroom, where she was taking a nap. When she woke up later, she didn't remember anything about it."

Even with everything I had experienced with demons, her story sounded fantastical. It was easy to see why other people had trouble believing what I said about demons and the power of the occult.

We talked more about it, then I left to spend time with Kurt at his house. His girlfriend was working, so I let my hair down and told him about married life in Texas. Kurt was all too willing to listen and offer comfort.

That night after I returned, Matt grilled me. "You were gone a long time. Where were you all afternoon?"

"Seeing friends," I said defensively.

"Was Kurt there?"

"Yes, we got to talking. I lost track of time."

It was true that we had only talked. But I couldn't lie to myself. The old attraction was still there.

Matt let it drop but stayed mad for the rest of the trip and beyond. After that, the fighting never stopped. Matt daily demanded to know who I had called and what I had done. I knew I had brought this on myself, but I couldn't stand the cross-examination. After a while, I dreaded the sound of his key in the lock. He drank more often, got mean when he drank, and attended church even less. We couldn't agree on anything, and his temper got more violent, even with Rachel. It was Idaho all over again. I was hanging on by my fingernails. I needed someone to talk to.

I found an AA meeting nearby and met Alexis. We became instant friends. I told her what was going on, and she suggested Al-Anon, which is the sister group to AA for family members of alcoholics. I wasn't convinced Matt was an alcoholic, but I went anyway. The other wives shared stories similar to mine and confirmed that it was up to me to change, rather than expect Matt to do all the changing.

Alexis also suggested I find work outside the home. A new restaurant was hiring waitresses, and Alexis needed a second job. We both applied and were hired.

Matt wasn't thrilled but knew I needed some adult time away from home. I hired a friend's daughter, Stacy, to babysit when our shifts overlapped. The only problem was that my training started on the same week that Matt's mother, grandparents, and siblings were coming to our house for a visit.

* * * * *

"What are you doing?" I asked Eileen, Matt's mother.

Matt's family had arrived the night before. This was our first morning together. Matt and I had slept on the living-room sofa bed. His grandparents, Ida and Clarence, took our bedroom. Eileen and her kids bunked with Rachel and Nick. I had just gotten dressed and was planning to make breakfast. Eileen beat me to the punch. Something was already cooking while she swept the kitchen floor; a chore I had been meaning to do.

"What does it look like? This floor is a mess."

"I was going to do that after work."

"You're leaving?" she asked. "We just got in last night! You should be spending the day with us."

"You're right. I'm sorry; I thought Matt told you. I just got hired. Training starts today. It won't take that long, and I'll have the rest of the week to do things with you guys."

Her eyebrows furrowed. "Matt took time off from work for us. You should do the same." Turning away, she attacked the floor with new vigor.

A minute later the grandparents emerged. They weren't happy either.

"You didn't leave towels out for us," Ida said. "We had to find them. Cheryl, a proper hostess always lays out necessary items for their guests. Didn't anyone teach you that?"

I was failing as a hostess on all counts. "No; sorry. I'll do better."

"*Humph.*"

She turned to help her daughter, Eileen, cook breakfast for the family while I grabbed cereal and left.

Each day of their visit, tensions mounted. Eileen and Ida found frequent fault with my homemaking skills, including the menu. They were used to three large meals a day with all the trimmings. I had grown up on simpler fare, and we were still on a tight budget. Matt thought my clothes were too revealing for his family. And so it went. Little by little, their collective remarks tore at my heart and chipped away at my self-confidence. I tried to conform, right up until the great family showdown.

We had just finished supper and it was my turn to do the dishes. Suddenly, the family started circling in the next room, with Matt in the middle.

"All those letters!" Ida shouted. She looked at Matt while pointing at me. Drawn like a moth to flame, I abandoned the dishes and approached the firing line. Ida, flanked by Clarence and Eileen, shot me a glare.

Instinctively, I stood beside Matt.

"What letters?" I asked.

"Oh, please! *You* wrote them! Telling us about everything but the money you owed us!" Her face trembled.

I looked over at Matt, surprised that he didn't seem confused at all. "Matt, what is she talking about? What money?"

"As if you didn't know!" Ida challenged.

Matt let out an embarrassed laugh and then faced me.

"They loaned us money to move to Texas. I was going to tell you as soon as I knew we could pay them back. But that took longer than I hoped."

"Oh, and while we're at it," Eileen chimed in, turning to me, "what kind of mother goes traipsing off to another city to work, leaving her newborn behind? You abandoned your baby!"

Now I was mad. "Matt, my mother loaned us plenty of money to move to Texas, and she never set a limit. Why would you ask your grandparents for more? And tell your mother that going to Los Angeles to work after Nick was born was *your* idea!"

"Oh, that's right; blame your husband," Eileen said. "Like you had no choice?"

Matt looked at me imploringly. "I was scared we wouldn't have enough money for the U-Haul, and first and last month's rent. I wanted a cushion." Then he faced Eileen. "And, Mom, she's right. I made her take that job. I didn't know how long I'd be out of work after I left the military, and I knew she could make more in Los Angeles."

"That's not what you told me then," she insisted.

My heart was breaking at his humiliation. All his secrets were being exposed. But how could he have thrown me under the bus like that?

"Cheryl, I'm sorry I didn't tell you about the loan. And Grandma, I should have written to you myself. I just kept putting it off."

Silence filled the room as we all realized the kids were watching and listening in the next room.

"This is some mess!" Clarence said, eyeing Matt and me. "You two better get your stories straight. Mother, let's go to bed."

The elderly couple shuffled off while Eileen gathered all the kids and retired for the night. That left Matt and me alone to face our sins. No wonder his family had arrived acting like they had a chip on their shoulders! The sheer magnitude of the miscommunication that passed for a marriage in our home was staggering. I saw no way forward from there. The next morning, days ahead of schedule, the entire clan packed up and left. It was a sad end that left us all regretful and angry.

After that, we tried to repair the damage but it was tough. Matt was ashamed that I now knew all his secrets, and I had a hard time believing anything he said. But it was a new season and there was much to do: I received my waitress training; Rachel was starting first grade soon; and Nick was adjusting to his babysitter. I needed to focus on that. I had no time for the black cloud filling our home. Even so, I felt myself pulling away from Matt. He responded with cruel words, name-calling, threats, and sporadic outbursts to keep me from leaving. Sabbaths got harder, too, as his temper escalated; he scared the kids with his erratic driving and sudden rages. Satan was orchestrating every battle, pitting us against each other as we escaped to our separate worlds. We were under attack. I just never dreamed it would extend to the youngest member of our family.

One evening after work I found Rachel upset.

"Mommy, Stacy hurt Nick today."

"What do you mean? How?"

"She spanked him hard. He cried a lot."

This was unbelievable. He was two years old and very compliant. What could he have done? I went to his room. He was napping. He looked fine until I pulled back the diaper, revealing bruises and welts. I immediately fired Stacy and rebuked her mother. Then I called the restaurant and quit. No job was worth that.

Without work, the problems at home magnified. In a last-ditch effort, I searched the phone book for counseling services. They were all too expensive or weren't taking new clients. A Catholic priest specializing in marital counseling agreed to see us. His services were free. I made an appointment, which Matt tried to cancel at the last minute. I told him our marriage depended on it. We needed help.

Matt went but wouldn't answer any of the priest's questions. I made a second appointment, but Matt later reneged.

"I'm not going back," he said. "You can, but I'm not talking to some guy I don't even know!"

I tried to change his mind, but Matt wouldn't budge. Days later, the final nail sealed the coffin. I was sick in bed with cramps and a migraine, unable to make breakfast. Matt stormed into the bedroom, holding Nick in his arms.

"Get up! The kids need you."

"I can't," I pleaded. "Can't you take care of them this time?"

Matt looked disgusted, then smiled wickedly at Nick, who innocently smiled back.

"Mommy won't make breakfast for you today," he said menacingly but still smiling. "Mommy's a #@&*. Isn't that right?"

Nick, unaware of Matt's intent, giggled. "Yeah. Mommy's a #@&*!" he said with glee.

My heart broke into a million pieces.

Matt pointed to the window facing west.

"If you're this unhappy, why don't you just go home to your parents? Leave!" Then he walked away, still holding Nick.

The following week Matt flew home to California for a wedding. While he was gone, I read books on marriage and divorce and the causes and patterns of escalating anger. I couldn't forget Matt's hateful words, telling me to leave. Closing the last book, I prepared to do just that.

I called my mom and asked if the kids and I could come for an extended stay while I sorted out our marriage. She sounded mysteriously reluctant, but agreed.

"This isn't permanent, right?" she asked. "I mean, you plan on getting some things ironed out and then going back to Texas, right?"

Her voice sounded strained; I chalked it up to concern over our marriage.

"Yes, Mom, this is only temporary."

Soon the plan was in place, the plane tickets bought. Despite all that, some expired registration tags on our car nearly derailed the trip when I got a traffic ticket. I got around this by going to night court weeks before my hearing date. A sympathetic judge let me pay the fine and be done with it. Nothing was going to stop me.

* * * * *

"Promise me you won't leave without saying goodbye," Matt said earnestly.

Rachel had just left for school. It was time to drive Matt to work. Boxes of clothes and other items had already been shipped to Los Angeles. I was preparing for an extended stay.

"I said I would," I replied. We had already discussed my plans for the day: shopping, lunch with Alexis, sedating Candy for her ride in the cargo hold, then signing Rachel out of school at dismissal time and getting Matt from work.

"This is just a separation. Right?"

I nodded. The kids and I would spend thirty days in Los Angeles at my parents' house while I got counseling and Matt got help for his drinking and anger issues. Tisha would stay with Matt.

Matt had made one final effort the Saturday before, taking me out for dinner at a fancy restaurant. He promised that if I stayed, he would do everything under his power to make things different. Unfortunately, I had heard it all before. This time his words bounced off my ears, never reaching my heart. I needed proof of this change from a respectable distance.

"I'll pick you up at three, in time for takeoff."

By eleven in the morning, we were done shopping and ready to leave the mall for my farewell luncheon with Alexis.

"Mommy, I have to go potty," Nick said.

Minutes later we were exiting the restroom by the customer service desk. I pushed the heavy door open with one hand, holding Nick's hand with the other. The door slowly began shutting behind us while we chattered about lunch. When it was almost shut, Nick inexplicably threw his other hand back behind him, right into the space between the door and the jamb. In that split second, the door malfunctioned and slammed shut, trapping his finger. I immediately shoved it back open, just as Nick screamed in pain.

Blood was everywhere. The door had torn Nick's fingernail from its bed. I started to drop everything to pick him up, but the girl working at the customer service desk ran over and scooped him up first.

Then she started to run.

"Follow me!" she shouted over her shoulder.

We ran through the store and mall, all the way to an emergency room for shoppers. Once inside, the girl gently put Nick on an examination table and filled in the doctor, who did a quick exam.

"I can sew the nail back into the nail bed so he doesn't go through life without a fingernail, but he'll have to wait. A little girl just came in with a broken thumb. I have to set it, then it's his turn."

That took two hours. We missed lunch, and I had no way to call Alexis to explain. I went straight to Rachel's school, just in time for dismissal. Then I ran home for Candy, leaving no time to get Matt or call him. The plane was leaving in thirty minutes.

I raced to the airport and through the terminal, throwing my car keys at the startled gate employee.

"Give them to my husband!" I cried. As the last passengers to board, we ran through the door to the jet bridge just as they were closing it.

On the plane, I resolutely pushed away my regret and self-recriminations and let God know that I knew He had used the malfunctioning door to keep me in Texas, just as He had used the traffic ticket.

It won't work, I silently prayed. *I'm going and that's that. You can't stop me!*

* * * * *

When we arrived at the lake house hours later, Candy ran straight into the fireplace to hide in the ashes. It was a tough transition for us all.

"Your dad comes back from his trip in a month," Mom explained, sounding nervous. "You may as well know, he won't be happy you're here. Now that he's retired he doesn't like his routine being disturbed for any length of time. If this separation lasts longer than that, we'll have to play it by ear."

I didn't know what she meant by his routine. I made no promises, just hoped that something would change in the next four weeks.

CHAPTER

14

nowing we would be in California for several weeks minimum, I registered Rachel at the local public school. California's laws allowed her to be in the second grade, but it seemed unwise to push her up a grade on top of everything else, so she stayed in the first grade.

With her settled, I found work as a restaurant hostess, put Nick in preschool, and called the United Way counseling center. They offered counseling on a sliding scale, making it affordable enough for Rachel to see her own counselor about the separation.

All went smoothly for a while. Then Satan came knocking.

It happened one clear, crisp afternoon when my mom was walking Nick to the guesthouse. Nick saw something odd. He told me about the event after I got home.

"Mommy, there was a man in the tree! He smiled at me!"

"A man? What kind of man?"

"He was big and fat and looked like a rainbow. Red and green and blue—lots of colors. I showed Grandma where he was sitting, but she couldn't see him. Why couldn't she see him? He was right there!"

Mom shrugged at my questioning look. "I was pointing out birds. Nick suddenly got excited and pointed up at the pine tree by the old glider. I couldn't see anything unusual, so we kept walking."

"Are you sure you saw a man up there?" I asked him. At his solemn nod, I knew what he had seen. The demon was back, this time parading as a colorful, jolly fat man. "Well, never mind. I'm sure whatever you saw is gone now. Come, let's read a book with Rachel so Grandma can go make dinner."

Throughout our stay, I tried to create normalcy and hoped to see some progress with Matt during this time. When Matt called, he always wanted us to come back but said he disliked AA meetings and didn't want a sponsor or counselor. His problems were nobody's business but his own. Disappointed, I made no plans to return.

At Thanksgiving, Matt and Alexis came for the weekend. On Thanksgiving afternoon, we were getting ready to go with my parents to Betty and Winn's house when Mom came to the door.

"I'm sorry, but you guys have been uninvited. Betty just called. They're uncomfortable with the situation between you and Matt."

My parents went to Betty and Winn's without us, so the five of us had Thanksgiving at a coffee shop. It was the first of many rejections to come. It was an uncomfortable weekend overall, with Matt losing his temper over small things and Alexis getting caught in the middle. When it was time for them to fly back, the kids cried, unable to understand why Daddy was leaving without us.

When our stay reached the two-month mark, my dad spoke up one night and laid down the law, demanding to know how much longer we would be there.

"I don't know," I said. "Why?"

His eyes were hard. He sipped his wine, then gestured to the kids. "Every time you go to a meeting, you put them to bed in the guest room. Then you leave it a mess until you need it again. That happens two or three times a week. I'm tired of it!"

I was burning the candle at both ends, and all he cared about was an unmade bed.

"I'm sorry, Dad. I know you don't like messes. I'll work on it."

"You'd better. I have a lady friend who comes every Tuesday while your mother's at work. I need that room clean for her—with the bed made! So either stop using it Monday nights or clean it up before Tuesday morning. Otherwise, you can find somewhere else to live. Understood?"

My blood went cold. Mom was cooking dinner in the next room. Surely she had heard him. He had never been faithful but bringing a woman into their own home was unthinkable. Furious, I told him I would never keep the bed neat for his mistress. He shouted more threats. I shouted, too, hurt by his attack. In the midst of the melee, Mom moved the kids to the kitchen and closed the door.

Dad's eyes never left mine. "*This* is why your marriage is in trouble," he said venomously. "You never think of anyone but yourself. You've always been selfish. That's why you left Matt to fend for himself. It's all about you, isn't it?"

Anger rose like bile in my throat. I wanted to defend myself and strike back. I opened my mouth, but words failed me. The same old, awful verbiage of the accuser that had spewed from Matt and Carl were coming from my own father, repeating what I had heard growing up. I had no defense against them. He held all the power, and I felt helpless in the wake of his cruelty. I knew his taunts were intended to deflect his own grievous sin, but that didn't matter. He could throw us out into the street.

"One more thing," he said with his eyes blazing. "I just want you to know I've been tape recording this entire conversation. That way when you and Matt wind up in court, he'll have irrefutable evidence that you're an unfit mother with a bad temper. Got it? So remember, keep that room clean. No excuses."

My eyes filled with tears of outrage. Without another word, I grabbed the kids and some food and walked out the back door.

"Mommy, what's wrong?" Rachel asked. "Why is Grandpa being mean to you?"

I waved her words away, unable to focus on anything but escaping that house. About halfway to the guesthouse, Mom caught up with us on the dimly lit path.

"Cheryl, don't worry about his threats. I have a plan."

I stared back. "Plan? What kind of plan? You heard him! If I don't keep your house clean for that concubine, we're out!"

She looked embarrassed but wasted no time on the absurdity of the situation. "I've been putting my own money aside for a year now. I was planning to leave him. This just speeds things up a little. He can't do anything if we leave first. I'll find something for all four of us. You'll see. It will be fine."

"Is that why you hesitated when I asked if we could come to California for a visit?"

"Yes. I wanted to help but knew you were walking into a snake pit. That woman's been coming for a long time, and your dad's drinking has gotten much worse since he retired. I finally had enough." She looked down sadly, then straightened up with a forced smile. "I'll find a place soon. Meanwhile, don't say a word. Just do what he wants. We'll be gone soon enough."

I should have felt relief; we were safe from eviction. Instead, I wanted to curl up and cry because I realized there was no safe place to go. The mess I had left in Texas was nothing compared to the one I had stepped into in California. Satan had covered every angle.

But life went on. I went to work. The kids attended school. The bed in the extra room was made no matter what. In early December, Matt sent roses for our anniversary, making me wonder if I should just go home and leave Mom to her own mess. In the end, I did nothing. Trauma had made me numb.

Before I knew it, the Christmas holidays arrived, and Matt came for another visit.

The four of us spent Christmas Eve Day at Disneyland, excited to see the Christmas tree in Town Square and other decorations. Even the horses wore shiny jingle bells. Before hitting the rides, we toured the shops on Main Street, including a jewelry store where I spotted a gold ring with a freshwater pearl. When we'd married, he'd had no means of buying me an engagement ring. So this time, I hinted, then cajoled Matt to buy it for me, but he calmly refused, saying it was too pricey.

I sulked for hours, angry that he wouldn't spoil me even a little. I knew he had gotten a raise; we could afford one small luxury. Despite my punishing attitude and frequent cutting remarks, Matt never bit back. He kept his cool all day, throwing me even more off balance.

When the four of us woke up Christmas morning, the kids came out from the closet where they had slept to tell us big news.

"We saw Santa last night!" Nick said with excitement.

"You did?" Matt asked, amused. "Where?"

"Daddy, we really did see him," Rachel insisted. "We were all sleeping when a noise woke me and Nick up. We looked through the slits in the doors, and we saw him—Santa Claus! He was looking at our presents, then he saw us and waved."

Amazed at their tale, Matt laughed out loud. Both kids immediately provided more details and a vivid description. Matt good-naturedly went along with it, then reminded Rachel that at the age of six, she was too old for making up stories. I knew better. Like the man in the tree, this was no story or game. It was serious business. I had never told Matt about the demons in my past and didn't that day either. He didn't need more ammunition. I was just glad we would be moving out soon, which was something else I couldn't tell him.

Mentally pushing all that aside, I joined in the fun of opening presents. Soon, there was nothing left but piles of torn wrapping paper and several new toys for the kids.

While they played with their treasures, Matt came over, carrying a small box.

"I have one more present for you," he said, a twinkle in his eye.

Surprised, I opened it. Inside was the coveted pearl ring.

"Matt, how did you get this?"

He laughed, tickled at his own plan. "When you took the kids to the bathroom, I ran back and bought it."

"But I never saw a bag or a box . . ."

"I know. I stuffed it in my boot."

I pictured that hard, square box inside his boot while we walked for hours throughout the amusement park.

"That must have been so uncomfortable," I said, deeply ashamed at the memory of my sour mood.

"It was worth it," he said simply.

"Thank you, Hon," I said, giving him a warm hug.

His sweet surprise carried us through several fairly harmonious days, but then the old issues surfaced one by one, exposing his persistent temper and putting me on edge. When Matt's visit was almost over, Dad convinced him that a family outing with him would be great fun. He wanted to visit Marineland of the Pacific, without Mom.

All the way there, I sat in the back seat with the kids, listening to Dad and Matt trade snide comments about my character and laugh. By the time we arrived, I was too angry to leave the car. I told them to go in without me. A stream of cajoling remarks followed until I had little choice but to comply. It was the only way to quiet their sardonic comments and placate the kids.

It was a miserable day, despite the picture-perfect weather and stunning views of the ocean. The kids wanted to see everything. My petulant heart wasn't in it, but I followed along. Finally, Dad urged me to let bygones be bygones. "Come here," he challenged with a loud laugh. "Let's have a hug and a kiss!"

I looked imploringly at Matt. He knew I didn't like being touched by my dad. He said nothing. Strangers milled around us. Music filled the air. This was no place for a scene. I felt sick doing it but forced myself forward like a lamb to the slaughter, dreading his embrace.

"Atta girl!" he bellowed, pulling me in. Then he grabbed my head and planted a very inappropriate, forced kiss on my mouth. My revulsion was immediate. I was twenty-seven years old, not the little girl he had messed with years before.

I shoved him off as hard as I could. "Don't ever do that to me again!" I shouted, not caring who heard.

"What?" he laughed, acting innocent. "It was just a kiss!"

"Stop," Matt told me. "You're scaring the kids."

Dad clapped his hands together. "Who's hungry?" he asked in his Grandpa voice.

The kids were happy to be sidetracked. "Me!" they both chimed in.

That night I tried to explain my feelings to Matt, but he wouldn't listen. He couldn't believe my dad would do anything inappropriate in public or private and said their barbs in the car were just teasing.

"Act your age, Cheryl. Grow a thicker skin. You've always been way too sensitive."

It was impossible to reconcile that the same man could plan a wonderful surprise for me at one amusement park, then annihilate me at another one just a few days later. Which was the real husband? For that reason, his departure at the end of that week was a relief, though the bereaved kids still couldn't understand his coming and going while we stayed behind. We weren't getting anywhere. Something had to change.

* * * * *

By January, Mom found us an apartment not far from Rachel's school. The move was traumatic. Dad raged at Mom's departure and blamed me. The stress was so bad that I suffered what the doctor called a migraine of the body. It took weeks to feel normal again.

The new season brought other changes too. Mom bought me a gently used car to replace the one I had been borrowing from Dad. I went back to college, which meant Rachel needed afterschool care. The solution was to put the kids in a combination preschool and afterschool day camp in the Santa Monica Mountains. It was perfect until a viscious crime ruined everything.

The day started out like any other. After school, Rachel and her classmates rode the bus to the end of the road where she and the other campers walked across a bridge to camp while a smaller group went into the woods to their commune. All the campers arrived just fine, but Rachel's friend and classmate never made it home. The boy was stabbed to death in the woods not far from the commune where his family lived. After that, Rachel struggled to feel safe and grieved the loss of her friend.

I tried to tell her that Jesus still watched over her and that God was still in control. She wasn't convinced. She said a teacher at camp had told her God didn't exist and religion was a lie. Rachel didn't know who to believe or where to turn. She wanted her old life back with two parents, her own room, and a safe school bus to ride every day. I wanted that for her too.

It all became too much. I needed help to sort out my life, so Mom helped pay for a counselor who specialized in sexual abuse and marital problems. I hoped to heal old familial wounds and make things right with Matt. Like Rachel, I missed being a family in our own home. Matt agreed to see the new counselor with me on his next visit to Los Angeles.

We had both come into the marriage with baggage: Matt from a broken home, and me from experiencing sexual abuse as a child and a lack of love and nurturing. I found counseling very healing. Matt found it unbearably personal. After one visit, he refused to go again.

We were out of options. I went back to Texas that summer without the kids to ship my furniture and belongings to Los Angeles. I stayed with Matt in his new apartment, and he took time off from work to help me pack. Ultimately, we talked. We went dancing. We swam in the apartment complex's pool at midnight. Without the stress of work, kids, and my parents, we were amazed to find ourselves falling back in love. I abandoned the packing and left with plans to return in a month with the kids to see if we could get along as a family. There was hope.

We came for a two-week stay, filling Matt's one-bedroom apartment to the brim. Thankfully, he still had the pull-out couch for the kids to sleep on. Matt had recently completed his training period and gotten a substantial raise. No more probationary period. His job tenure was secure. Giddy with financial security, we traded in our old car for a brand-new Ford Bronco and hit the road for a family road trip to San Antonio.

At first, it was fun. The kids loved being back in Texas with their dad. We ate out, went swimming, and visited the Aquarena Springs amusement park in San Marcos. It was also hot. The kids got grumpy and bickered. Patience wore thin in the motel room. Matt wasn't used to dealing with them 24-7. I wanted proof he could cope and control his temper. He wanted proof I would stay for good.

The euphoria faded, and we started fighting again. The last straw was when Rachel got frightened by a bee and accidentally stepped on Matt's boot. His reaction was swift, mean, and physical. I immediately shut down. I had seen enough. I took the kids back to Los Angeles. With help from Alexis, my furniture and belongings soon followed.

The following spring after countless lines had been drawn in the sand, I threw in the towel and started dating again, then filed for separation. At the same time, I found a new doctor for an old problem. The same menstrual pain I had experienced for years had gotten much worse. A laparoscopy confirmed that endometriosis had spread throughout my abdomen. The doctor ordered a hysterectomy to cure the problem for good. The news made me wonder if this was God's punishment for my rebellious heart or merely Satan making good on his penchant for revenge. I knew my behavior was out of line, but I still felt like a spiritual punching bag. I wanted to be left alone.

Matt came out for the surgery, and I was glad for the help. But several weeks later the trial for our legal separation took place without him or a lawyer to represent him. Any threats from my dad about using tapes to help Matt win custody had evaporated. I received child support and alimony that allowed me to focus on school without needing as much help from Mom.

As the spring of 1987 wound down, I realized something was still wrong. The doctor hadn't warned me that the sudden lack of hormones would be a shock to my system. I was only twenty-eight years old and still needed hormones, but the organs that produced them were gone. The world literally looked dark, as if the sun were eclipsed. I suffered insomnia; hot flashes; mental fuzziness; headaches; night sweats; nightmares; and a deep, overwhelming sadness I couldn't explain. The spark and energy I had always possessed naturally had been removed with my organs.

On top of that, I also started having severe abdominal pain and a fever. When the pain and fever got intense, I called my general practitioner. She sent me to the hospital, where a young surgeon diagnosed me as having appendicitis and immediately operated. In addition to the appendix, he also removed staples left behind from the hysterectomy and pieces of ovary with gangrene that had spread to the appendix.

The doctor said I would be fine after that and should have no more pain. She was wrong. Within weeks, it came back. It was later determined the endometriosis was still growing and forming adhesions that required more hormone treatments. I was on a roller coaster, trying to rid my body of the same persistent disease.

During that time, I somehow managed to graduated from the community college and had a tempestuous affair with Jesse, who was a member of AA. He was exciting and attentive. But like the others before him, he soon got abusive, repeating the accuser's same old, vicious patterns. When our relationship ended, the pendulum swung back to God's side. I took a hiatus from dating and focused on school, the kids, and my friends from AA and church.

That was also a rough year for Rachel. She got in frequent trouble at school and was often unhappy. She was angry at my romantic and domestic instability and lashed out with disruptive behavior that escalated. In response, I reacted too harshly and demanded a level of godliness and order that even I couldn't achieve, though I constantly tried. Perfection was the goal; but it was an impossible goal that left failure and heartache in its wake, frustrating all of us.

The most obvious area of contention for Rachel was school. I had received frequent calls from her third-grade teacher, who complained of her disruptive behavior in class. I had her tested and discovered she was hyperactive and possessed a near-genius IQ. She was tested for the school's gifted program but didn't quite fit their requirements; she was brilliant in some areas, while average in others. They were looking for consistency. In addition, her classmates picked on her for being too talkative. Public school wasn't a good fit for her anymore.

It was also time to get out on my own. For two years, I had slept in the living room while Rachel shared a bedroom with Mom. Only Nick had a room to himself. We needed more space.

When Nick graduated from preschool, the kids and I moved to a townhouse that was close to an Adventist school, and Mom moved into the guesthouse at the lake. That fall Nick started kindergarten and I registered for classes at a nearby university. Rachel skipped fourth grade to be with kids her own age. At the age of ten, Rachel could already read faster than I could and devoured thick books before we could even get them home from the library. Because she was so bright, it was hoped that more challenging work in a smaller, safer environment would help her concentrate better, avoid trouble at school, and maybe even calm her down at home. I felt sure a new place and new school would provide the fresh start we all needed and would improve the relationship between Rachel and me.

At the same time, I was equally convinced that romantic relationships meant abuse for me, arrows from the accuser, and inevitable failure, so I avoided them, even though deep down I still wanted the love and acceptance of a man. The problem was finding a man that wouldn't caress me with kisses one day and leave a bruise on my arm or heart the next. Spiritually, the pendulum remained out of balance. How often had it swung from wild abandon to unattainable perfection and back again? I seemed to go from mistake to mistake and longed for a secure, solid, satiating salvation that eluded me. In the end, I felt that God wasn't any happier with me than I was with myself. I had lost my way, and Babylon was on the horizon. Pain and sickness were becoming an everyday part of life, which made me a recluse.

Eventually, I took an indefinite medical leave from the university and stayed home. I concentrated on trying to get well and create the solid, consistent relationship with God that I had wanted for so long. I was sure the answers were out there if I just kept looking. But Satan lurked in every corner, even tempting me with a brief reconciliation with Jesse. I quickly ended the romance again, this time for good.

* * * * *

One morning I woke up in pain from my most recent surgery. There had been several as doctors tried to find and eliminate the source of my ongoing abdominal pain. This was my first night at home after the surgery. I got up for a pill and almost went to the upstairs bathroom for tap water; it was just steps away. But I wanted cold water from the fridge. That unfortunate decision led me to the stairs.

I stopped at the top of the stairs. The house was dark. Both kids were asleep. I grabbed the railing with my right hand, eyeing the top step in the glow from the bathroom night-light. A drinking cup was in my left hand. I waited for my eyes to adjust. Then I felt it: an evil presence surrounded me. I ignored it as pain seared through my abdomen, demanding attention. I didn't have time for demons.

I lifted my right foot to prepare for that first step. In that split second—with my foot hovering in midair—an unseen force hit me hard from behind. My feet flew out from under me. High in the air like a helpless doll, I fell. My hand still held the railing, but it was no use. When I came down, I fell in a prone position and was unable to stop myself. The stairs were cement and rock, covered with thin, loose carpeting. The edge of each step was hard. Landing flat, my spine hit those edges in several places, before I tumbled down the stairs.

For a minute, I couldn't move. More pain shot through my abdomen, and I prayed no stitches had come loose. Eventually, I got up slowly and went to the kitchen for water, then back upstairs to check the stitches. They looked fine, so I went back to bed.

The next day my back was sore, so I went for X-rays. There were no fractures, so I went home.

At first, I was grateful I hadn't been injured. Then slowly things changed. Besides the same old abdominal pain, I felt an odd tingling up and down my right thigh and experienced back pain whenever I sat on the floor. Then more pain shot through my groin and right leg. Tests were run. One doctor diagnosed this as neuropathy. Another said I was nuts. Deep down, I knew I had been hurt on the stairs and berated myself for putting cold water above safety and common sense. Even so, I knew I had not fallen on my own. My old enemy had pushed me down those stairs.

* * * * *

Months passed with no definitive diagnosis for the ongoing abdominal pain or symptoms in my back and right leg. I was underweight with practically no appetite. The smallest task left me exhausted. I was becoming an invalid and barely able to care for the kids. During school hours, I rested in bed or in the garden. At night, I slept fitfully. One night I dreamed we were having an earthquake. It was bad enough to make the wall behind Nick's headboard collapse to the ground below while he screamed for rescue. The next morning I wondered if it was just a random dream, a warning from God, or Satan's attempt at scaring me. I had been having a lot of nightmares and often felt the presence of demons at night.

After that, I pored through the Scriptures every night for answers. I wanted to know why I was so sick all the time and why I had so much pain. I felt riddled with illness to the point of being unclean. I was still young but rarely went anywhere or saw anyone. I was an unhappy recluse, cut off from the world except for the kids' school and church. I wanted to know how I had gotten to that point and what I needed to do to fix it.

One night it all came to a head. Like other nights, I had spent hours wrestling with God while the kids slept, unable to rest until I knew why God was ignoring my pleas for healing. Then something happened. One by one, the verses revealed a pattern. Some were convicting:

"The women of Zion are haughty,
　walking along with outstretched necks,
　　flirting with their eyes,
　strutting along with swaying hips,
　　with ornaments jingling on their ankles" (Isaiah 3:16).

Others were soothing:

"For I know the plans I have for you," declares the Lord, "plans to prosper you and not to harm you, plans to give you hope and a future" (Jeremiah 29:11).

"Nevertheless, I will bring health and healing to it [Jerusalem]; I will heal my people and will let them enjoy abundant peace and security." (Jeremiah 33:6).

"Do not be afraid. . . .
You will forget the shame of your youth
　and remember no more the reproach of your widowhood.
For your Maker is your husband. . . .

The LORD will call you back
    as if you were a wife deserted and distressed in spirit—
a wife who married young,
    only to be rejected," says your God (Isaiah 54:4–6).

If God was to be believed, He was now promising to restore my health and be my Husband in lieu of the husband who had rejected me and was now dating someone else. While it made sense, there still wasn't a clear answer on how to receive this healing.

Frustrated and worn out, I cried out to God. "Why won't You heal me?" I said aloud, with my arms upstretched and eyes turned toward heaven. "What do You want from me?" When no answer came, I dissolved into tears.

In the midst of my weeping, a still, small Voice reached my heart. *"What have you done for Me?"*

Petulance flared up fast. "What have *I* done for *You*? I go to church every week! I tithe! I read the Bible with Rachel and Nick and pray with them every night. I keep all your rules. I even stopped dating men who don't honor You. I'm alone in this world; my family wants nothing to do with me, and I have no husband. And still I serve You! What more do You want?"

Again came the still, small Voice: *"What have you done for Me?"*

I wept, stricken with sudden understanding. He wasn't asking me to give up more things or follow more rules.

"Father, how can I give You anything? I can't hand You a gift. I can't kiss Your robe. I have nothing to give and no way to give it to You."

A profound silence followed. I strained to listen and to know God's heart. Then, like the first faint wisps of smoke from a fire, the answer came. He brought to mind the story of the woman in Luke 7:36–50 who anoints the feet of Jesus with perfume and her own tears in gratitude for His forgiveness. I had been forgiven too. It was time to say Thank You.

"Lord, how can I do what she did? You aren't here."

"I am the Word."

According to John 1:1, "the Word was God." So the Bible in my hands *was* Jesus, as surely as the Man Jesus was there with the sinful woman who anointed Him in person.

"OK. You're right. I have the Word and that *is* You. But I have no perfume."

"Yes, you do."

He was right! I had forgotten that the women at my church had given me a small bottle of real perfume. In that moment, I knew what He wanted me to do.

The clock read 2:00 A.M. It was a school night.

"I understand, but it's late now. I need sleep. I'll do it tomorrow."

I closed the Bible and turned out the light. In no time, I started to fall asleep. Then a car backfired outside. I grumbled, turned over, and was falling asleep again when the cat pounced on my feet. I shooed her away. In the dark, I again told the Lord I would keep my promise *tomorrow*, then burrowed into the pillow. Then the cat knocked something over.

"All right!" I said, sitting up. "I'll do it now!"

I fetched the perfume and closed the door. I got my new burgundy leather Bible with the onionskin paper and fine binding. That was everything I needed. I knelt on the floor in a prayerful pose and took a deep breath before the throne of God.

"Lord, I'm sorry I put You off. You're right. Some things need to be done right away. No delay." I sighed while thinking. "Father, thank You for saving my life when I was young and foolish and was involved with drugs and promiscuity. You saw the promise of a better life and a sweeter heart in me when no one else did. You knew that if I found You, I'd serve You for the rest of my life."

Tears of shame and gratitude started flowing.

"I'm sorry I've let pride get in the way. Please forgive me for chasing after men when Matt rejected me. You are my Ishi* God, my heavenly Husband. I know You want the best for me and not the worst. You are great and mighty, merciful beyond measure. Lord, please accept this offering. Let it be pleasing to You. I love You, Jesus, with all my heart. This is for You and You alone."

I opened the Bible and poured the entire contents of the bottle along the Bible's center, from top to bottom. To my surprise, the perfume instantly disappeared into the pages and binding, with nothing running out of the ends. It was simply gone. There was nothing left to do, so I put everything away and went to bed as my mission was accomplished.

The house was quiet, including the cat. Satisfied the house would stay quiet, I shut my eyes.

"I hope You're pleased, Jesus. I hope You liked it. Am I done now? May I go to sleep? Praise be to You, Lord. Amen. Good night."

After that, all the stress and the strain left me. The sweet sensation of sleep enveloped my entire being. The bed was a soft cloud, allowing me to float away.

---

* See Hosea 2:16. In this instance, the Hebrew word *Ishi* means "husband."

And then it came: Wave after powerful wave swept through me, through my head and out of my toes like a warm, liquid electric current of love. If I had been a filament, I would have lit up the room with the Shekinah glory of God. The offering had been accepted. This was His miraculous thanks; God reciprocated my outpouring of love as only He could. Each wave left me awestruck; each as powerful as the one before. The waves continued for several minutes as I lay there completely still, not daring to move except to smile in tearful gratitude. It was an infilling of the Holy Spirit like nothing I had ever experienced before. It was magnificent.

*   *   *   *   *

The next day I still hurt. I felt no better than I had the day before. In short, I had not been healed, but now I knew that He was listening. If I kept at it, surely He would lead me to a diagnosis and cure.

I soon found a new neurologist. He immediately took a new tactic of common sense.

"I think you have a broken arm and the flu," he said with a grin.

"Pardon me?"

"Metaphorically speaking," he chuckled. "What I mean is, I believe you have two completely different things going on, rather than a single ailment that can explain all your symptoms. I'm going to order an MRI of your back. The rest should be checked out by a good gynecologist. I'll give you the name of someone I trust."

His recommendations made total sense. I followed them to the letter.

The MRI revealed two herniated discs at the base of the spine where I had hit the steps. The gynecologist performed another surgery and found another staple on the underside of my tailbone, lodged prong-side up. Every time I sat down, I landed on those prongs. The surgeon removed it, and the pain was gone. As soon as I recovered from that surgery, an orthopedic surgeon went in to fix the herniated discs, but mistakenly repaired only one. I would need more surgery.

At that same time, Mom came down with pneumonia and started having mini strokes. She needed help. Thankfully, she had plenty of assets and a healthy retirement. Getting a place that was big enough for all four of us wouldn't be a problem. Finding one she liked would prove to be a little harder.

CHAPTER

15

"I don't want to sleep in a den," Mom said.

We were touring a 1950s ranch with a realtor. The acreage had mature trees and a barn and needed minimal repairs. The price was low, so Mom could pay cash. Except for the nearby freeway, it was perfect. Its only drawback was no fourth bedroom, just a den off the kitchen.

"Mom, it's away from the kids' rooms, has big windows, and we can add doors for privacy. You'd have the biggest room in the house, with no steps to worry about."

"No! I want my own space, away from everyone else." Mom made her point, despite her speech getting thicker by the day. The strokes were making it harder for her to talk and communicate, even though she was only seventy-four years old.

I swallowed a sigh. She had always been gentle and soft spoken while I was growing up. Lately, though, her personality had taken a sharp left turn. She cried over little things and often lost her temper with the kids. Now she was being stubborn about how much house we really needed.

"OK, Mom. It's your money." I turned to the realtor. "Do you have anything else?"

"There's a house in the foothills that's still under construction. It will cost more, but it has separate 'granny quarters' just for her." She touched Mom's shoulder. "Would you like to see it today?"

"Yes," Mom said forcefully.

We drove for ten minutes to a quiet little enclave with a quirky mix of homes. The house we had come to see was a split-level on a hill overlooking the valley, with a park and a horse ranch nearby. It had three bedrooms upstairs and the kitchen and living room downstairs. The granny suite was by the garage and just two steps below the foyer. The house was beautiful—everything we could ask for. It was also one hundred thousand dollars more than the smaller ranch. That meant a mortgage, which my mother hadn't dealt with in years. They had paid cash for the lake house.

"I like this one!" Mom announced. "How soon will it be ready?"

"The first of January. Will that work?"

A sick feeling filled my stomach. This house was too much, too big, and too expensive. What if Mom's health failed and she needed a nurse? I still needed one more back surgery and didn't know when I would be able to work. With interest rates topping 18 percent, the payments would be monstrous, plus the taxes and insurance.

"Mom, are you sure? It's so expensive! I know we can make that other house work just fine."

"No!" She slammed down her cane. "I want this one!"

The realtor shot me a look. "I could set up a meeting with the builder and draw up the papers."

Mom looked at me with determined, if slightly rheumy, blue eyes.

"I need to see your father. Take me there tomorrow."

* * * * *

Dad was against buying the new house. "It will go into foreclosure; you'll see. Why don't you just buy me out of the lake house? It's too big for me anyway. I want a condo."

The lake house was the cheapest solution, and I loved the lake. But it only had two bedrooms plus the guesthouse. I couldn't sleep out there again. The kids were terrified of seeing more demons and were too young to be out there alone. Mom loved the guesthouse, but it was cold in the winter and the path was dangerous. One fall could kill her.

Finally, I took it to the Lord.

In a hurried, haphazard attempt, I prayed for guidance, closed my eyes, let the Bible fall open, and stabbed blindly at the page. My finger rested on Haggai 1:15: "The Promised Glory of the New House." That's all my eyes saw—the new house. I didn't read carefully and missed that this book actually warns Israel *not* to focus on their own houses, but on God's house first. Because I didn't know Scripture well, I missed the true message and thought God was telling me to go ahead with the new house. It was a classic error of the biblically illiterate: "My people are destroyed from lack of knowledge" (Hosea 4:6).

Another verse I didn't consider: "Honor your father and your mother" (Exodus 20:12). My father had clearly said No to the new house. While my mother opposed him, she was too ill to know what was best. Because Dad had been so unloving in the past, I rationalized that I could circumvent his fiscal wisdom and get a different answer from my heavenly Father. In truth, I had gotten the same answer from both. I just didn't realize it at the time.

For these reasons, I took Mom's side. She bought the new house, mortgage and all. We moved in January 1990.

For a few months, life was a series of doctors for her and pain management for me, while the kids adjusted to another move. We all loved the house and the rural neighborhood, but Mom's health steadily declined as winter gave way to spring. By summer, Mom had her fill of doctors and tests. One doctor discovered she had breast cancer and removed the breast but quietly told me the cancer wouldn't kill her. Instead, the dementia, which was causing her diminished memory, difficulty swallowing, unsteady gait, poor appetite, garbled speech, confusion, and mercurial emotions, would kill her first.

We did our best to find things for her to do, such as riding a special bus to the senior center for lunch and joining the kids for trips to the library. Each morning at breakfast she'd get tired of reading the backs of cereal boxes and would switch to reading every Adventist magazine and pamphlet that came in the mail. Soon, she asked to go with us to church, Sabbath School, or both.

Leave it to God to use boredom and a lack of secular reading material as evangelism tools! I was delighted and took her to church as often as possible.

She also watched more religious television, including a movie on the life of Jesus during Easter week. The scene at Calvary made her cry, further opening the door to faith. And one day just for fun, we borrowed a friend's convertible and took mom for a drive with the top down, making her squeal and giggle like a school girl . . . a sound that was pure joy for us all.

One day she quietly announced she wanted to be baptized for her seventh-fifth birthday in September. Her late conversion brought joy to my heart, especially since her time was running out. She had turned her back on God for decades and now was returning to Him. I treasured the time we had left together.

That summer, I had a second back surgery, which was more extensive than the first. While I was in the hospital, Mom fell down the two steps leading to her suite. Her entire right side was bruised. I was heartbroken and scared.

As soon as I was discharged, I ignored the doctor's instructions for total bed rest and cared for Mom. She was now bedridden and needed help with everything. She choked on food and water, making her gaunt and frail. She knew who we were but couldn't speak well enough to be understood. Her staunch dignity was being cruelly stripped away.

In August, she asked to see our pastor. He spent an hour praying with her alone. Afterward, he came out to talk with me. "She gave her heart to the Lord today. You don't have to worry about her salvation. It's secure."

Four days later, just three weeks shy of her seventy-fifth birthday, she was gone.

*   *   *   *   *

While I grieved, there was work to do. Accounts were closed. Proof of death was needed so her retirement funds could be signed over to me. Her belongings were sorted and distributed or disposed of. It was a painful process, especially when I found the telltale signs such as shaky signatures and trouble with figures that revealed she had been struggling with dementia for years, long before anyone knew.

Even with the money she left me, there was no way to keep up the mortgage payments. By that time, I had been diagnosed with an auto-immune disorder that explained the chronic fatigue, poor appetite, low energy, body aches, and frequent bouts of illness. It meant that working a regular job was impossible at that time. I tried to refinance the home, but was turned down. The house had to be put up for sale. Unfortunately, the housing market had taken an unexpected tumble. The realtor said it was worth one hundred thousand dollars less than what we paid for it, less than a year before. Our finances were looking grim.

After Mom's death, Nick had trouble sleeping. The pastor had foolishly told him on the day of her passing that a demon might show up in his room pretending to be his deceased grandmother. Nick was only seven; instead of comforting him, this warning made him afraid to be alone at night. This was made worse when another seven-year-old boy was murdered not far from our house while Nick was outside playing alone. This put everyone in the neighborhood on high alert and further compounded Nick's growing list of fears.

On the bright side, not long after Mom's death, Dad came to make peace at last and asked to be part of our lives. I said Yes, as long as he kept his hands off me except for chaste hugs and didn't yell at anyone. He agreed and started coming for regular visits.

Meanwhile, a problem developed at church. I had firsthand knowledge that a wealthy, married elder was sleeping around with female members. Disturbed by this, I told the pastor what I knew and hoped he would do something to stop it.

A week later the pastor asked me to meet with him and two elders. I thought they might ask me for more details about the rogue elder. Instead, they said our church would no longer help with my children's school tuition. The school that the kids attended was under the umbrella of a different church across town. *Our* church funds were only supposed to support the school under its umbrella.

"What are you suggesting I do?" I asked.

"Ultimately, we'd like to see your children moved to our school. If you'll do that, then we're happy to continue helping with their tuition as long as needed."

"But Pastor, your school is thirty minutes from our house. Their school is just ten minutes away. We moved to be close to that school. They have friends there, and they're both doing well in class. It doesn't make sense to move them, especially midyear."

The pastor looked stern. "Nevertheless, if you don't change schools, we will withdraw our financial aid immediately."

"I can't move them. They've lost so much already!"

"Then I suggest you move your membership to the church affiliated with that school. That way they can offer financial assistance from this point forward."

"If that's what you want, I'll put in for the transfer right away."

"That's not necessary. Our church secretary will take care of that for you."

I left, fighting tears until I was alone. Then they flowed like a river. It was obvious I was being ostracized for speaking out against the wayward elder; his philandering continued long after the kids and I left.

Over time, we adjusted to the new church. It was nice that most of the children there were in school with my kids. But we all missed the friends we had left behind. Thankfully, about that time, a writing assignment came along that involved the whole family. I was hired to write a children's cookbook. To make the process more enjoyable, I encouraged the kids to help me think up fun recipe names and even test out each culinary creation. The book was a big hit, a feather in the cap for all of us.

Then came the next blow. Dad's health began failing, so he put the lake house up for sale and moved to a condo near my brother Tom.

Six months later I got a message on my answering machine that he had died from cancer. Dad and I had made peace, but unlike Mom, he died rejecting God. Around that same time, Uncle Winn died as well, but I was comforted knowing Winn had a strong, long-standing relationship with God. Still, my immediate family was shrinking fast.

Meanwhile, the tumultuous nature of the relationship between Rachel and me had only escalated through the years, reaching toxic levels for us both. For that reason, not long after Dad passed away, Rachel chose to go live with Matt and his girlfriend in Texas.

A few months later, I asked my new pastor's wife for prayer about my marriage. I felt certain I had made a mistake not working harder to heal it. She sent me to Polly, who was in charge of our prayer ministry. Polly took my hands and fervently asked God to stir up the nest of Matt's household and cause his girlfriend to leave—but only if He wanted Nick and I to move back to Texas for the reconciliation of our marriage and family.

Just days later, Matt called to say his girlfriend had left him! I immediately told Polly and in Gideon-like fashion, asked if we should really pick up and move. She angrily told me not to return to an abusive marriage. Clearly, she had not expected God to do what she'd asked. Her response scared me, and I lost my nerve. Nick and I stayed put. Matt's girlfriend soon returned and he immediately asked for a divorce so he could marry her.

I hired a lawyer, Mr. Smith, hoping the divorce would be simple and quick.

* * * * *

"It's hot!" ten-year-old Nick complained. "And I need a bathroom!"

He was right; it was very hot for January. We were at a car show in downtown Los Angeles, so I could write a spec article for a boys' magazine. Nick had been cranky all day and was getting more so. I tried to focus but soon gave up. I felt a migraine coming on.

When we hit bumper-to-bumper traffic on the 405 freeway, Nick started crying from frustration and discomfort. Fed up, I let loose with a fit of anger. In that moment, a tsunami of compounded despair from years of loss and constant struggling with man and principalities hit me all at once. Right there in the car, I grieved over losing both parents, my looming second divorce, and having the rest of my family turn away one by one. Not caring who heard me, I yelled that I was completely, totally unloved.

"I love you," came a small voice from the back seat.
That I knew. Still, I cried.

*　*　*　*　*

"Mom!"

On January 17, 1994, the morning after the car show, Nick's scream of terror came with violent shaking that woke me up. During the endless trembling, my television crashed, and the sound of breaking glass came from all directions. Anything that wasn't nailed down, including furniture, banged against the walls or fell over. Unlike my dream at the townhouse, this was the real thing. The house pitched and lurched like a boat at sea. The walls creaked and groaned while the bookcase and the dresser at the sides of my bed rocked back and forth, ready to fall.

"Don't move!" I screamed. My four-poster canopy bed was probably the safest place for me to be. In the new house, Nick's headboard was against an interior wall and away from the window. There was no point in trying to reach him during the shaking.

The moment it stopped, I yelled, "Stay there; I'm coming!"

I jumped out of bed and flew to his room, then we went outside and sat on the porch steps, feeling the ground tremble beneath us like a living animal. The whole neighborhood was awake, calling to one another and shining flashlights to look for damage. It was 4:30 A.M. Sunrise was two hours away.

"You guys all right?" Barney, our neighbor across the street, aimed a flashlight at us.

"We're fine. You folks OK?"

"Yep, no one's hurt. The place sure is a mess though." He handed me an extra flashlight. "Here, you'll need it to check the inside of your house. I'll go turn off your gas in case there's a leak." He turned, then aimed his light back at my bare feet. "Better get shoes while you're in there."

"You stay here," I told Nick. "I'll get your shoes too." He nodded, eyes wide with terror, struggling to be brave. "I'll be right back," I assured him.

Inside, the bright beam revealed a living room littered with books and knickknacks that had flown from bookcases and off the fireplace mantel. The kitchen was an even bigger mess. Glasses, dishware, and pantry items lay smashed everywhere. The refrigerator door had opened, spewing its contents on the floor as well. I turned from the mess to look upstairs for shoes and robes.

The stairs and the hallway were clear. I stopped at my bedroom door to sweep the room with light. To my horror, the mauve carpeting between the door and the bed twinkled like a sea of diamonds. Hundreds of glass shards blanketed the floor, along with several larger hand-sized chunks, which rested razor point up like vicious daggers lying in wait. The broken pieces were from the antique, leaded-glass lampshades for the lamps in my bedroom. Two more large glass table lamps lay in the rubble, miraculously unbroken.

My breath caught as I realized I had just run barefoot through all that glass! Maybe I was cut and didn't know it. I aimed the light at my feet and looked for blood. Nothing! Not even a sliver. Angels must have carried me across the room. Stunned by that revelation, I tiptoed around the glass and toppled TV to the walk-in closet for shoes. The closet floor was piled high with boxes and other items that had fallen from the shelves. Under the rubble, I found shoes and a robe, then grabbed the Bible I kept on the bed. Nick's room was next. It was a mess, too, with books, rocks, and other treasures all over the floor, but no broken glass.

I walked through the rest of the house, inspecting walls and ceilings. There were a few minor cracks in the drywall but nothing major. The new house had withstood the initial shock without structural damage. There was no smell of gas leaking. Satisfied that the house was intact, I went outside.

"Here," I said, handing Nick his shoes and robe before putting on my own. He was still right where I had left him. I sat down and put an arm around him. "We'll be OK; you'll see."

Unconvinced, he said, "I was so scared!"

"Me too," I admitted. "Earthquakes are scary. I went through another big one in the valley when I was about your age. Same thing—early morning, still dark, books and glass items flying all around me. My hamsters wouldn't stop squealing." That made Nick giggle. "But we got through it. No one in my family was hurt. We'll get through this one too. You'll see."

To comfort us both, I flipped on the flashlight and opened the Bible to read aloud. Before I could find a comforting passage, my eyes fell on a passage I hadn't read before:

> "Under three things the earth trembles,
>   under four it cannot bear up:
> a servant who becomes king,
>   a fool who is full of food,
> an unloved woman who is married,

and a maidservant who displaces her mistress"
(Proverbs 30:21–23, 1984 NIV).

I felt numb while reading those words to myself. I *was* an unloved woman who was married. I had said as much the day before on the freeway. And the earth still trembled beneath me. I took a deep breath and turned the pages for something more soothing to give us courage while we waited in the dark. Each time I thought it might be OK to go back inside, another aftershock hit, so we stayed put, talking and reading aloud, until the sun came up. Then we went inside to clean up and get things back to normal.

Severe aftershocks continued throughout the day; some were almost as big as the first quake. My friend Misty told us to come over to her family's house just up the hill; her neighbors were gathering to barbecue or cook on propane stoves the food that would soon spoil without electricity. I had already filled the cooler with ice and meat from the freezer, so we took some of that and Mom's old battery-operated, portable TV and hung out with them all evening. We gathered around the tiny TV and watched the news in horror. Entire neighborhoods throughout Los Angeles had been devastated. Buildings and freeways had collapsed, killing and injuring untold numbers of people. We also learned that the water main in our neighborhood had ruptured, which explained why we had no water.

We were blessed to still have a home. Several houses in our neighborhood were condemned. We had no electricity for three days and no gas for a week. We made do with oil lamps and blankets. It took three weeks to get clean water again. In the meantime, a kind man showed up every night with his own water truck, filling everyone's water jugs for free until he ran out. We drank it, cooked with it, and poured it into the toilets to make them flush.

The physical hardships and stress in the weeks that followed made my residual back pain unbearable and my autoimmune illness much worse. I felt bereft and alone, with no one to turn to or call. No parents. No husband. No family. They were all gone. Satan had systematically stripped my life of all the usual support systems. It was all up to me, and I didn't feel up to the job. To top it all off, the earthquake destroyed my lawyer's office, delaying our divorce indefinitely.

During this time, our house remained on the market. There had been few interested buyers from day one, but now no one came to look. Buyers were spooked by all the condemned homes in the area. Naturally, my financial reserves slowly ran out while I waited four years for the house to sell. In the end, just as Dad predicted, it went into foreclosure. Once again our lives were turned upside down.

In the fall of 1994, we rented a townhouse not far from the Adventist academy associated with our home church. By that time, Rachel had moved back in with me and attended the academy. This move did not feel like a fresh start. Instead, it felt like a dead end. The inheritance money was nearly gone, and my health still didn't allow me to work full time.

There were many times during the years that followed when Satan had me convinced that God had left the scene. Life was too hard. In addition to my parents, Betty and Winn were gone; both dying from cancer. Tom and Cindy no longer talked to me, nor did Ellen and her husband. My in-laws and other extended family had long since washed their hands of me and the kids. Eventually, the kids moved out, too, Rachel to live in her own place, Nick to live with Matt and his new wife.

I became convinced that the only explanation for such a Job-like existence was that I had simply made too many mistakes. I wasn't worthy of life's most basic comforts: a loving husband and extended family, a home of my own, good health, and financial stability. Each of these things had eluded me for so many years that the dream of ever attaining them had become nothing more than a cruel mirage—too elusive to touch, let alone attain. For that reason, salvation felt equally unavailable. If I didn't warrant love and happiness here on Earth, what made me think God would give them to me in heaven? The evidence suggested I was not worthy of any of it.

Satan had spent years tearing me up in every way possible. It was obvious that he thought I would give up in despair, and I almost did. I kept to myself and let the world carry on without me. I came to the conclusion that I would never feel safe, secure, loved unconditionally, and sure of salvation beyond doubt. All that was impossible.

But what was the alternative? Give in to Satan? Live his way? No. In my darkest moments, I still knew there had to be a way to belong to God without chronic fear and self-recriminations and without constant harassment from the enemy. It was in this darkness that I finally encountered and came into true relationship with the Savior.

EPILOGUE

"Would you be interested in attending a new Bible study?" Jean asked, absentmindedly brushing her blond bangs out of her kind blue eyes. Jean and her husband attended our church.

"What kind? Is it here at church?"

"No. It's a nondenominational study, just for women. It meets near the academy. We just started Genesis, so you're not behind. Here, I'll write down the address. Come next Monday morning at ten. I'll be there. We can sit together."

Jean's invitation sounded intriguing. It was a little scary; but I figured if it didn't sound or feel right, I would just stop going.

On Monday, I joined Jean and got started. That year we read every word of the Pentateuch. I loved discussing each week's lessons with women from different Protestant denominations, and I learned much as we studied the Bible each week.

Beyond the intellectual stimulation of sharing ideas and opinions, I also fell in love with the meaty concept of reading each book of the Bible in order, line by line, precept by precept, without jumping around or skipping over anything. For the first time ever, the Bible made total sense to me as the pieces of the story of Israel fell into place. Biblical names and stories were no longer disjointed characters with little in common. Instead, they formed a cohesive story line that laid out God's plan of redemption clearly.

When that first year of Bible study ended, I eagerly kept reading on my own, starting with Joshua, and then continuing on to the very end of Revelation. What began as a lukewarm appetite for spiritual knowledge steadily grew into an insatiable hunger to learn more about God and His Word, without relying on sermons to teach me. As I read, and internalized every word of that same burgundy Bible I'd once anointed with perfume (which I still use to this day), God's true, complete character and unfailing love became as clear to me as the story itself. In turn, getting to know God through His entire Word revealed who *I* was to *Him*, what He expected of me, and what He wanted *for* me. In short, as I saw God differently, I saw myself differently. I grew a new heart and let go of pointless, destructive legalism. I fell deeply in love with Jesus on an intimate level while discovering the ways of the Holy Spirit, tangibly feeling His love and presence and learning to hear His voice clearly.

It is true that early in life I missed out on a lot of wonderful opportunities out of fear, legalism, or both. But other opportunities came along. While the kids were growing up, I wrote countless stories and articles for Christian publications, determined to use my gifts for God. There were books along the way and other writing successes. With the kids grown and out of the house, I went back to school to earn my bachelor's degree in journalism, with a collateral in English, and found physical restoration in the university's indoor aquatic center. After that, I went back to work full time and then earned advanced degrees at a local Bible college. There I learned to stretch my wings through serving God in ministries that included creating and directing an annual women's conference and hosting a weekly radio show that highlighted local politicians and leaders in ministry making a difference for the Kingdom.

I also discovered the joys of volunteering at a pregnancy center where I co-led a Bible study for women recovering from abortion and spent several weeks helping women at a prison. I started leading a weekly Bible study for women at a local mission; something I've continued doing for six years and counting. I enjoy the challenge of teaching Sabbath School at my church when I'm needed to fill in for someone, and I am blessed to have a sweet group of ladies who come to my home every week for Friday night Bible study. Recently, I was delighted to discover that the hungry young man my friends brought home from Hollywood so long ago went on to be a Seventh-day Adventist pastor with a worldwide radio ministry.

Many relationships were also healed and redeemed when God restored and gave back what the enemy stole. I now have a strong relationship with both kids and am thankful that I live close enough to Rachel to see her often. Both kids are successful in their chosen careers, and I am proud of them. Several years ago God gave me the most wonderful, unexpected gift of Christian "God-parents" who live close by and love me unconditionally, sharing their prayerful wisdom without reserve. I also have two sets of godly sisters and brothers in Christ who are closer to me than my biological siblings ever were. I was blessed to join a Sabbath School class whose members have also become like family as we go on regular trips and outings for the sheer fun of it. And He gave me a rich, strong network of Christian friends, coworkers, and business acquaintances that make life infinitely easier and more enjoyable. My relationship with God has also deepened over the years as I have learned to empty myself through regular fasting and prayer. These practices never fail to open the gates of heaven and make the Holy Spirit's voice even more clear. I have learned to trust God with all things, from hopes to heartaches, including disasters like the one that narrowly missed burning down the lake house, only to burn down the homes of others. Now that I know His character, I realize that He is sovereign and never does anything by random chance. Everything He does is with purpose and part of His plan, which I now trust. That trust and closeness has made me as tangibly aware of being in love with Jesus as I am of my own breathing in and out. He is my Constant.

Like all Christians, Satan is still my opponent. But I no longer fear him or his demons. Over time, my relationship with God has grown so strong, deep, and intimate that Satan can't harass me anymore. Now I am truly a new creation, out of the enemy's reach. I can sleep at night without fear.

Ultimately, God was there all along. I just needed to put all else aside long enough to truly find the whole of Him, rather than disjointed bits and pieces of His character mixed with secondhand hearsay. Now that I have found Him, salvation is no longer a question. I'm free to put His will above my own and serve Him because I love Him, not because I am afraid to break the rules. I am safe in Him, not because of what I do, but because of who He is. I was a lost, rebellious, forlorn exile in the Babylonian desert of shame, illness, and despair. When I set out to consume all of Him, I became the spiritually healthy "good fig" I had always yearned to be:

> Then the word of the LORD came to me: "This is what the LORD, the God of Israel, says: 'Like these good figs, I regard as good the exiles from Judah, whom I sent away from this place to the land of the Babylonians. My eyes will watch over them for their good, and I will bring them back to this land. I will build them up and not tear them down; I will plant them and not uproot them. I will give them a heart to know me, that I am the LORD. They will be my people, and I will be their God, for they will return to me with all their heart' " (Jeremiah 24:4–7).